1001
Designs for Needlepoint
and
Cross Stitch

1001
Designs for Needlepoint
and
Cross Stitch

B. Borssuck

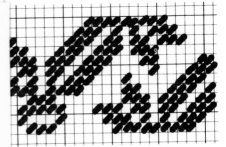

ARCO PUBLISHING COMPANY, INC.
NEW YORK

To
ALINE BLUMNER
with gratitude for her friendship
and inspiring suggestions.

All graphs and needlework by the author.
Photography by John E. Unbehend and Dennis Curatolo
of Photo-Graphic Arts, Syracuse, N.Y.

Published by Arco Publishing Company, Inc.
219 Park Avenue South, New York, N.Y. 10003

Library of Congress Cataloging in Publication Data

Borssuck, B.
    1001 designs for needlepoint and cross stitch.

    Bibliography: p.180
    1. Canvas embroidery—Patterns. 2. Cross-stitch—
Patterns. I. Title.

    TT778.C3B65   746.4′4   77-1701
    ISBN 0-668-04214-1 (Cloth Edition)
    ISBN 0-668-04222-2 (Paperback Edition)

Printed in the United States of America

Contents

I NEEDLEPOINT

II CROSS STITCH

List of Illustrations

I NEEDLEPOINT

II CROSS STITCH

For here they may make a choice of which is which
and skip from worke to worke, from stitch to stitch.
From *The Needle's Excellency*
by John Taylor (1580–1653)

I
Needlepoint

You have reason to be proud of your needlework if it is meticulously done; but when subject, composition, and choice of colors are all yours and yours alone, you also satisfy your urge for self-expression.

Every professional designer uses reference material. If you have had little or no designing experience you certainly need "something to rest your eyes on" while you dream about the pillow you want to make. But be assured that you are as much a designer when you combine traditional forms into pleasing compositions as when you create something outstandingly original. In either case, the results are uniquely yours and truly self-expressive.

This book contains my adaptations of classic and traditional ideas graphed for thread and stitch counting techniques. Items for which they might be used are numerous, ranging from small pieces such as pin cushions, watch bands, luggage tags, or coasters to large wall hangings and rugs. Only your own needs will limit their usefulness, your own imagination their adaptability.

Graph lines are all ten-to-an-inch for simplified calculations, but of course you may use any canvas or fabric you find suitable for your project.

The designs in the first part of this book were prepared primarily for working with the Half-Cross, Tent, Continental or Basketweave Stitches, as they are probably the most popular needlepoint stitches.

A symbol is used, rather than the solid block or outline style of graphing, because it results in a graph that most closely resembles a finished canvas done in Tent Stitch. Moreover, and this is very important when designing for Tent Stitch, the symbol method shows up any weakness in diagonals from upper left to lower right that might turn the finished design into a meaningless series of dots.

Graphs done in Half-Cross Stitch symbol may be used without alteration for doing Cross Stitch.

All bands and borders shown as horizontals can be changed into verticals by either of the two methods shown on page 104.

The photographs suggest ways in which to execute, vary, adapt, or enrich selected patterns.

I hope that these designs will be helpful to you, either to be executed as shown when they answer your decorating problems or used as reference material to spur your own imagination, creative ability, and craftsmanship.

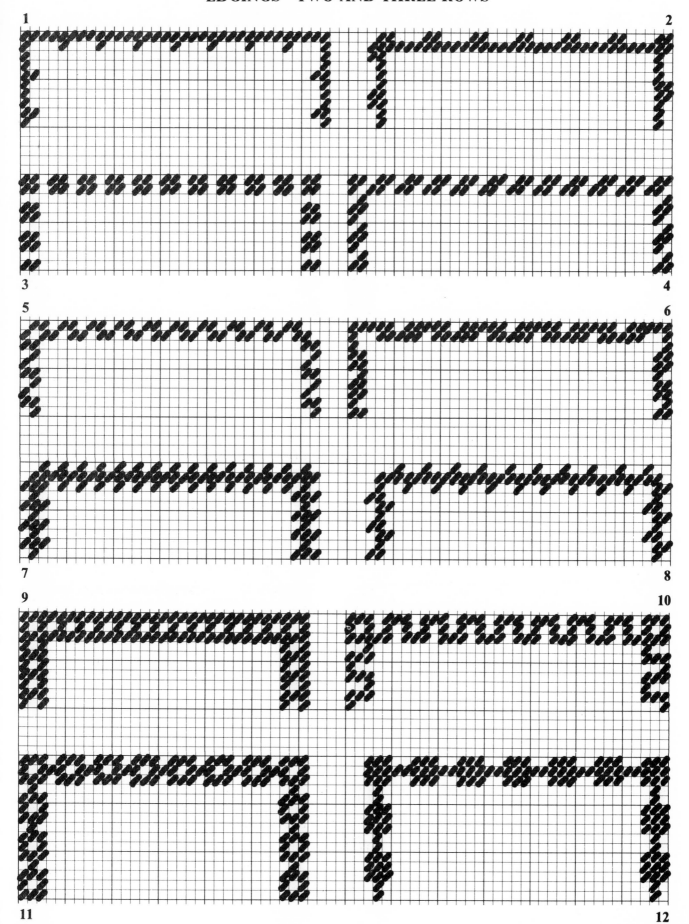

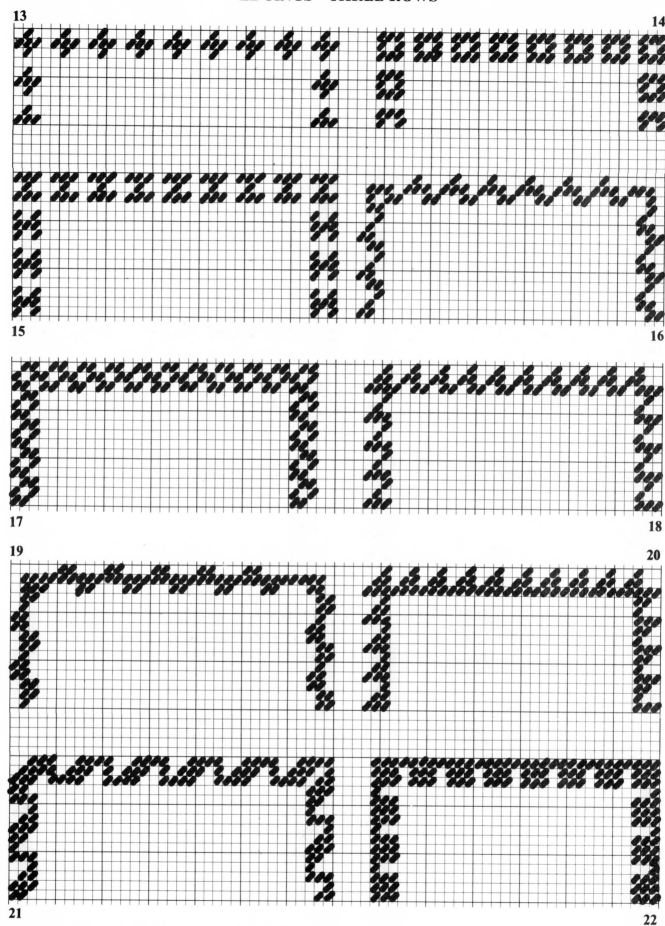

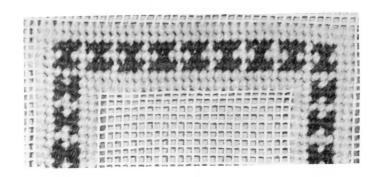

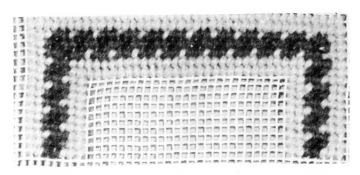

Designs 15 and 17 Simple edgings can provide an interesting finish for the background surrounding your picture.

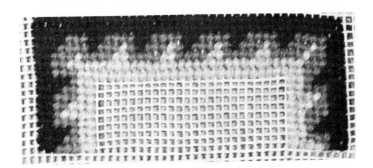

Design 21 Edgings may be used to soften or accent the contrast between ground and border.

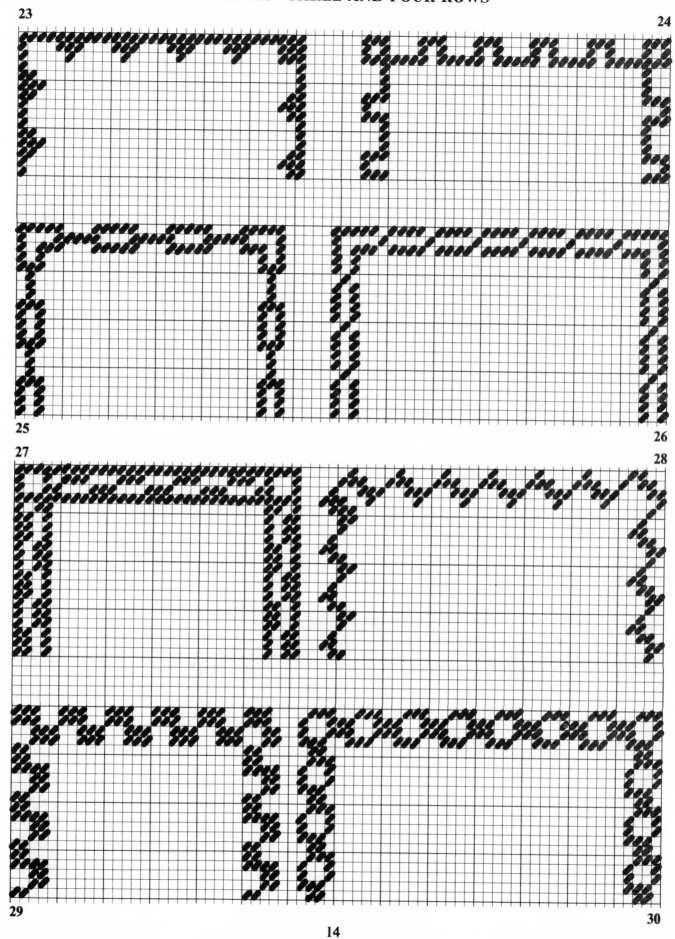

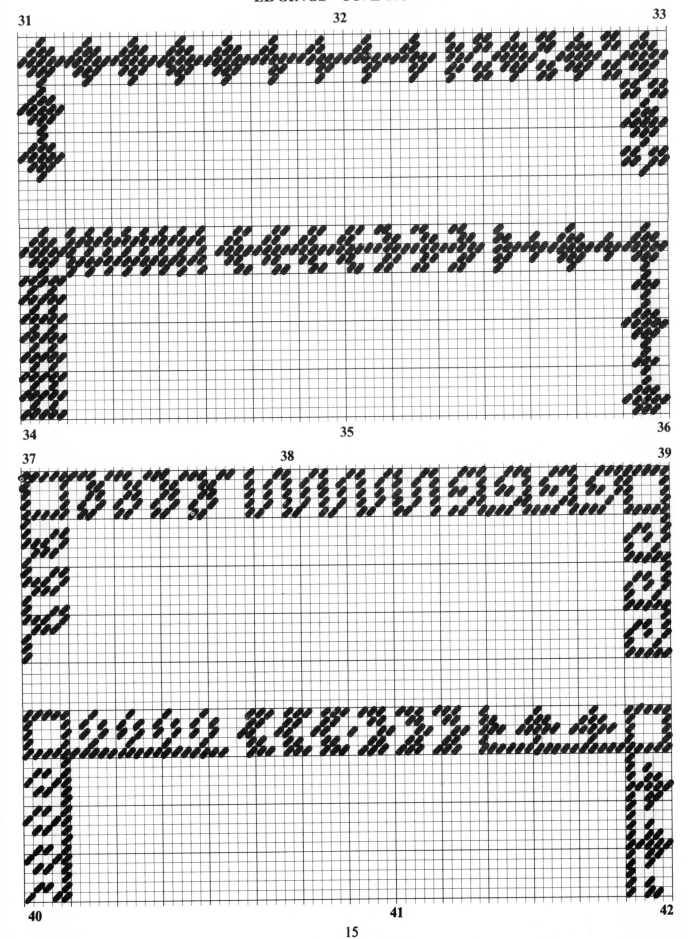

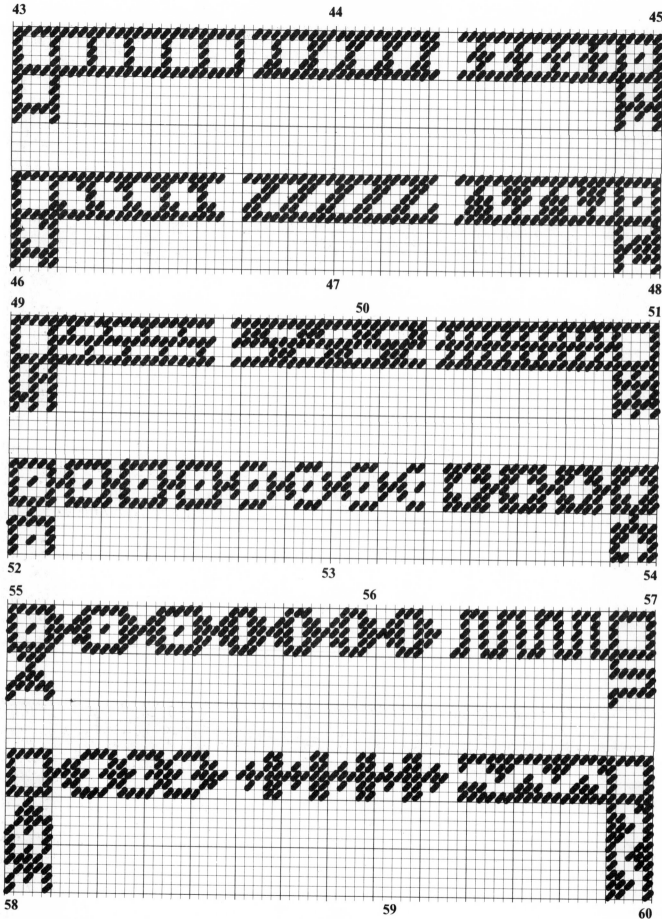

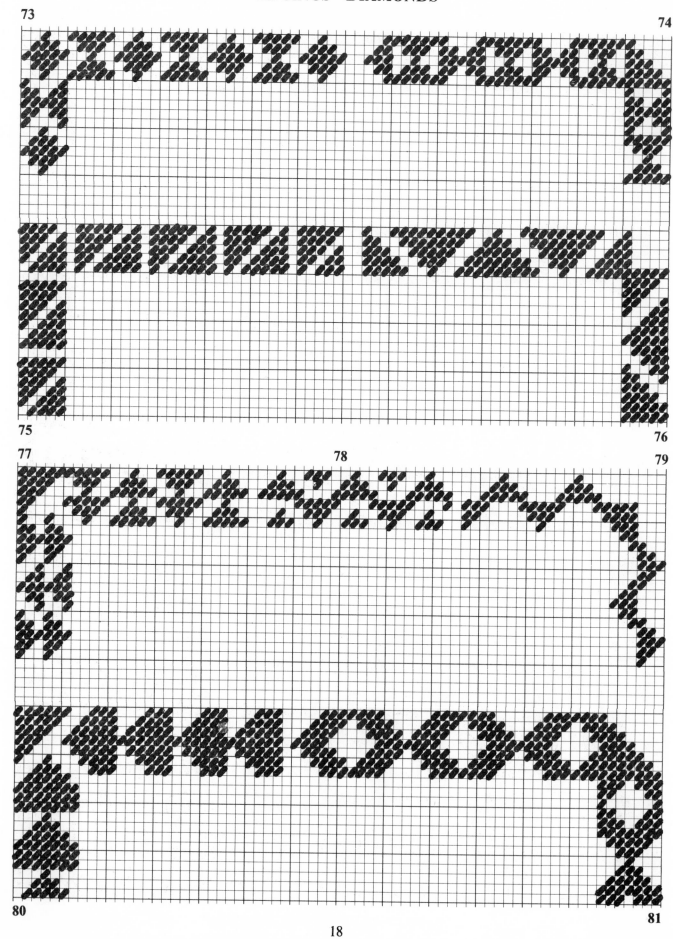

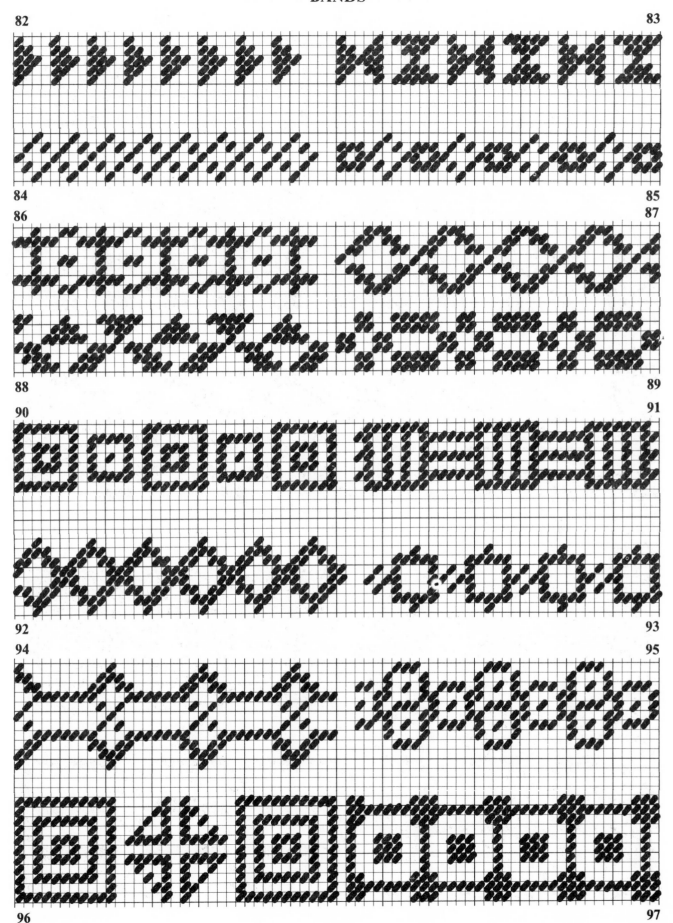

98   99   100   101

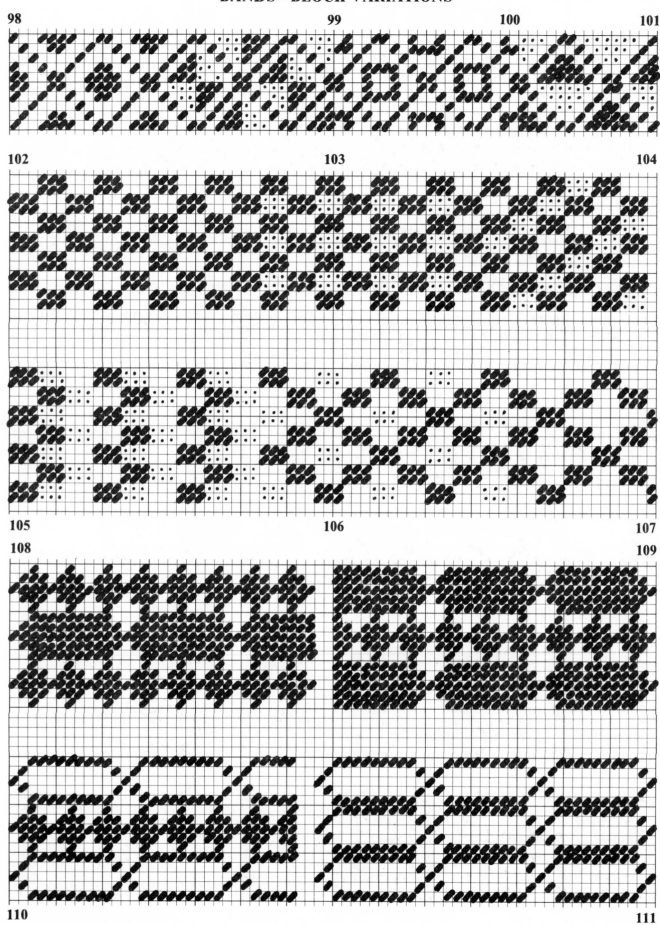

102   103   104

105   106   107
108   109

110   111

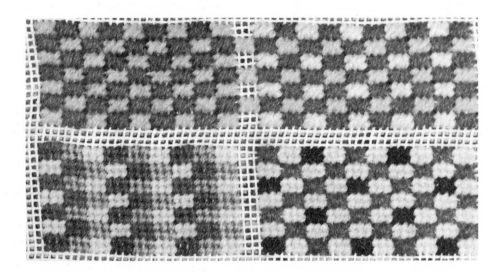

Designs 102 and 103 Mosaic Stitch gives a homespun look to this simple pattern.

Designs 105 and 106 Tent Stitch only or Tent Stitch and Smyrna Cross give a more formal looking texture.

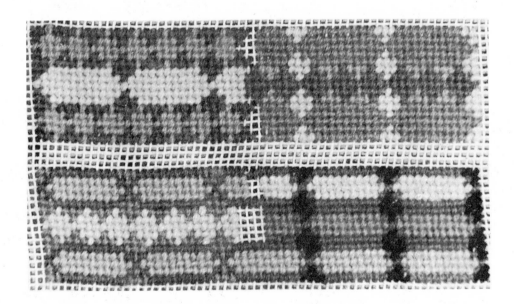

Design 108 and 110 The horizontal pull in the pattern as graphed has been maintained by the choice and placement of colors.

Design 109 and 111 Here a strong contrasting color (either white or dark) interrupts and balances the horizontal effect.

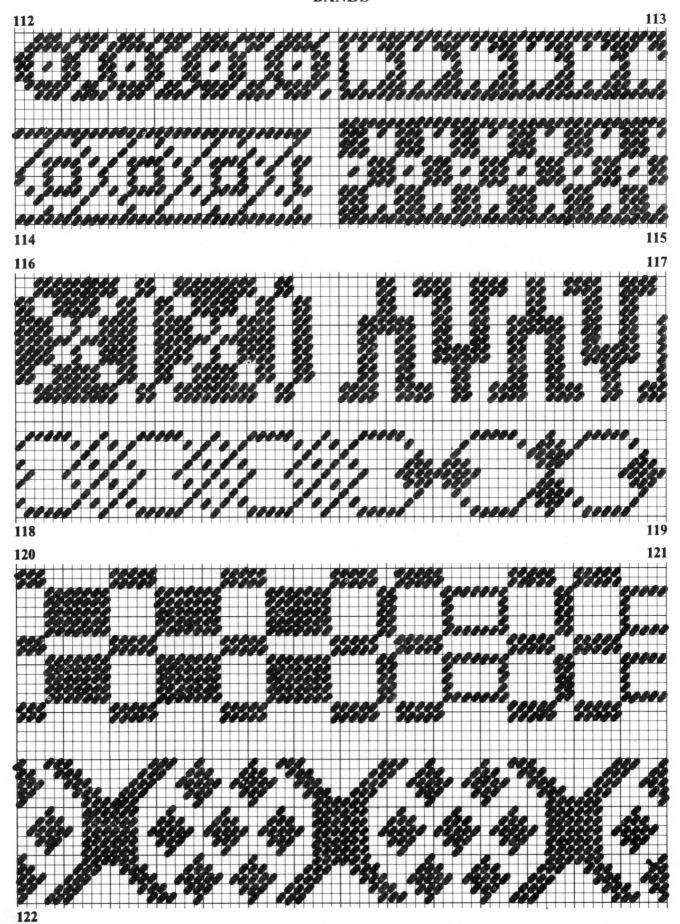

112

113

114

115

116

117

118

119

120

121

122

123 124

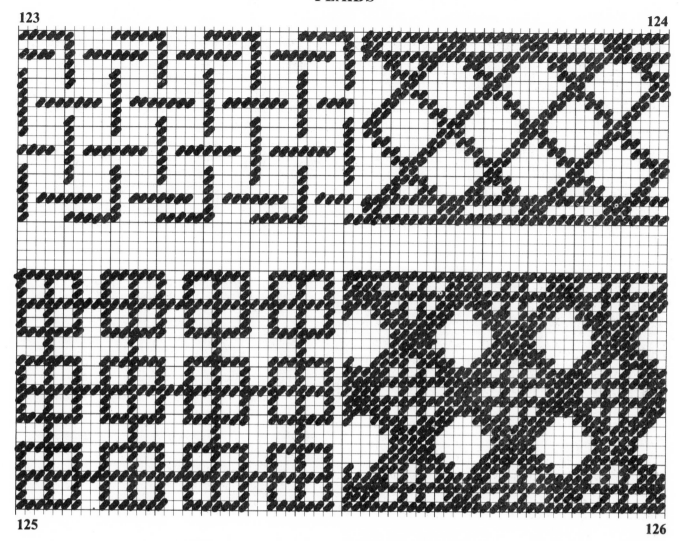

125 126

127 128

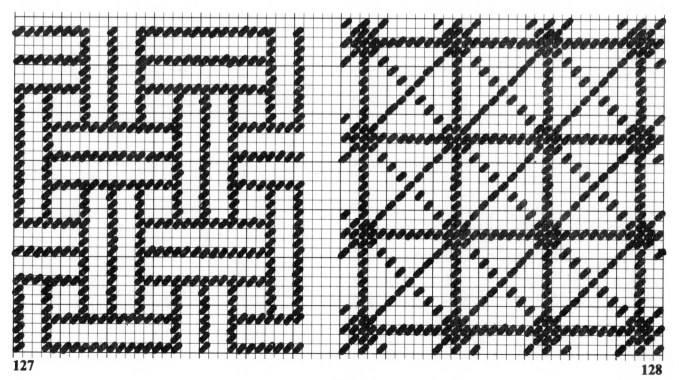

129

130

131

132

133

134

135

136

137

138

139

140

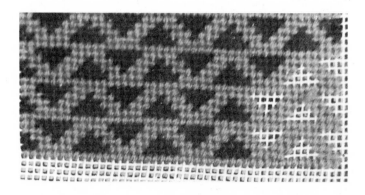

Design 139 As charted, in two colors, Tent Stitch.

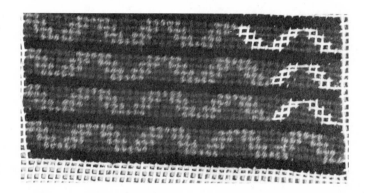

Design 139 A single row of Outline Stitch done in a darker color causes the ribbon-like effect.

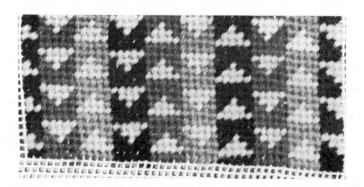

Design 139 An adaptation of the graph and the use of three colors result in vertical stripes.

141

142

143

144

145

146

147

148

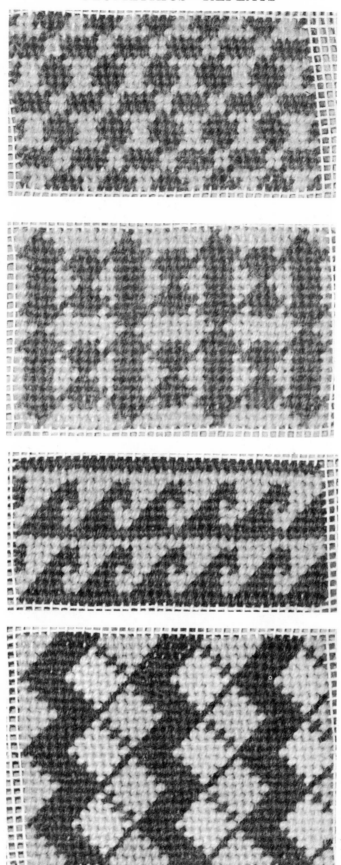

Designs 141, 143, 146 and 148 All-over designs such as these may be done in monotones for a soft, subtle look or in strong, contrasting colors for a vibrant effect.

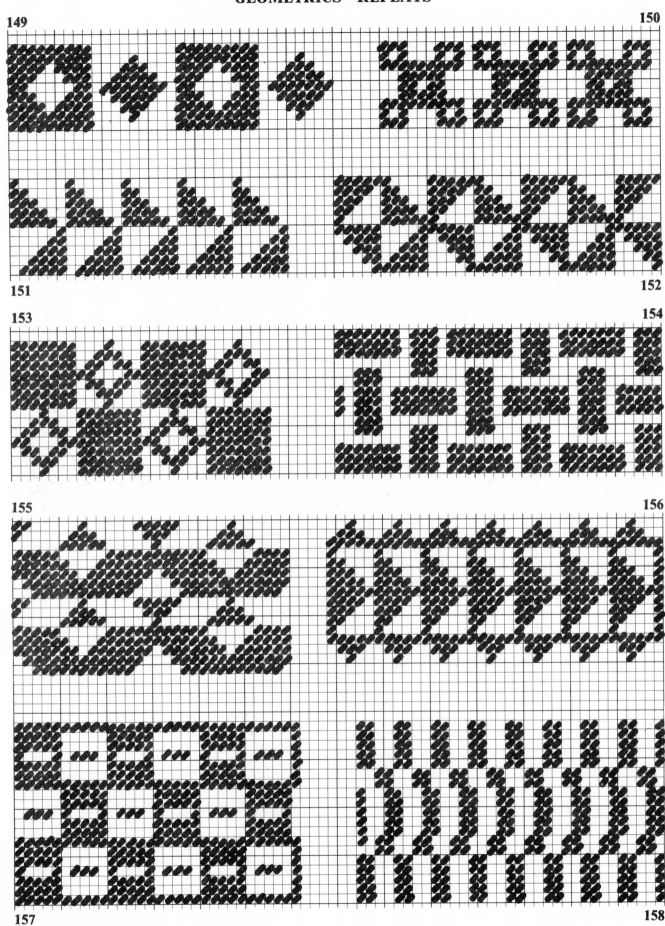

149

150

151

152

153

154

155

156

157

158

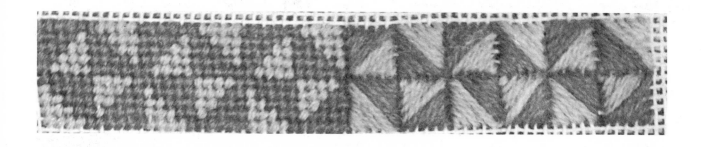

Designs 152 and 155 In Tent Stitch as graphed and in Cushion Stitch, demonstrating that the use of texturing stitches may alter the charted design beyond recognition.

159

160

161   162   163

164   165

166

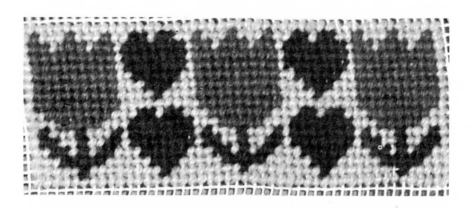

Design 161 Motifs are worked in color on a light background.

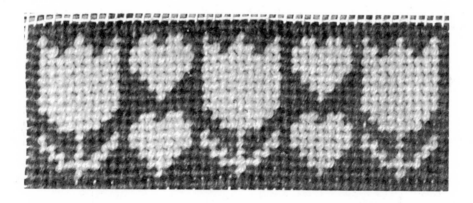

Design 161 Motifs are worked in white and the background in color.

Color or silhouette—the choice is yours.

167

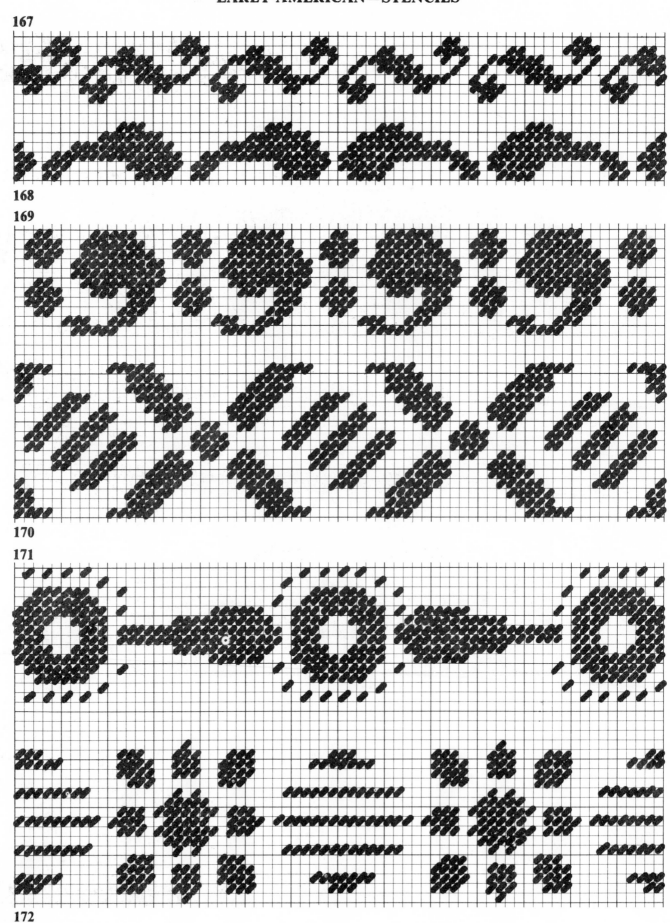

168

169

170

171

172

173 174

175

176

177

178

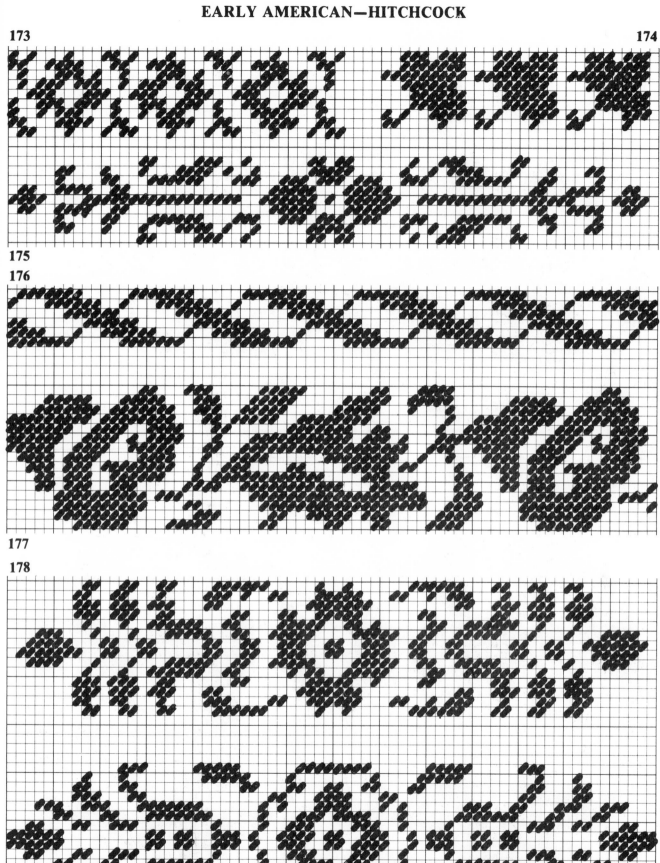

179

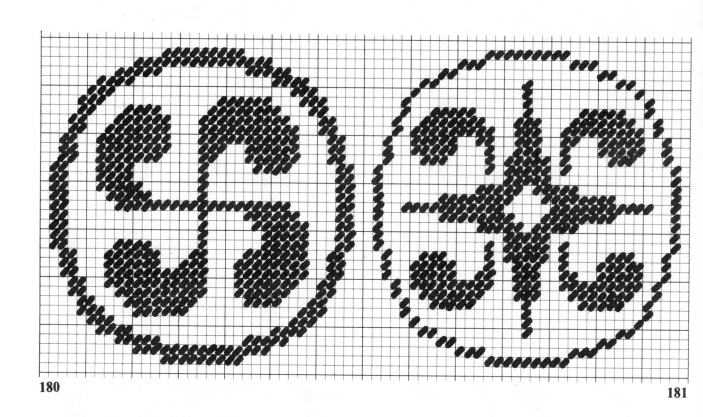

180   181

182   183

184

185

186

187

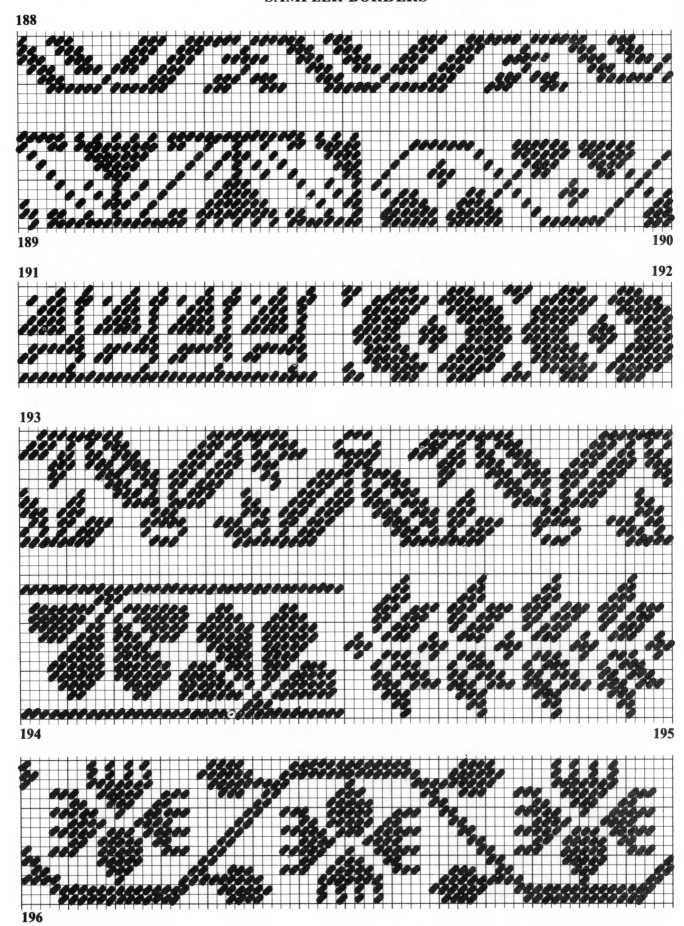

188

189

190

191

192

193

194

195

196

Designs 188, 193 and 195 Three designs were used to form this wide band. Repetition of a harmonious combination of several border and band designs can result in unusual and interesting all-over patterns.

197
198

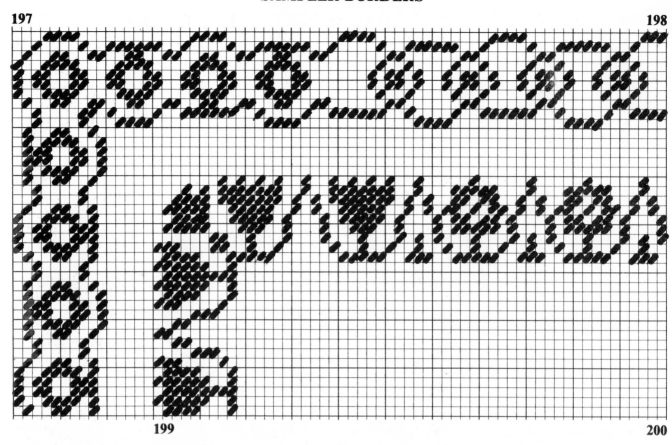

199
200

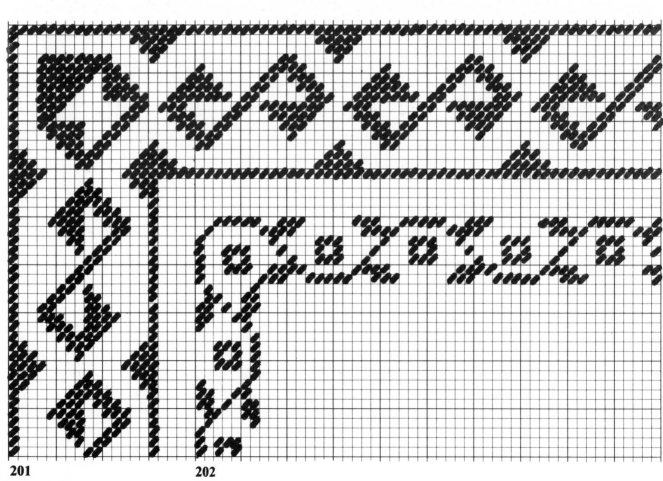

201
202

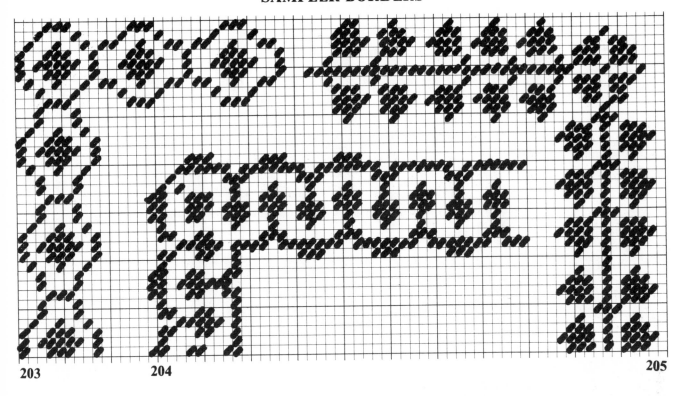

203   204   205

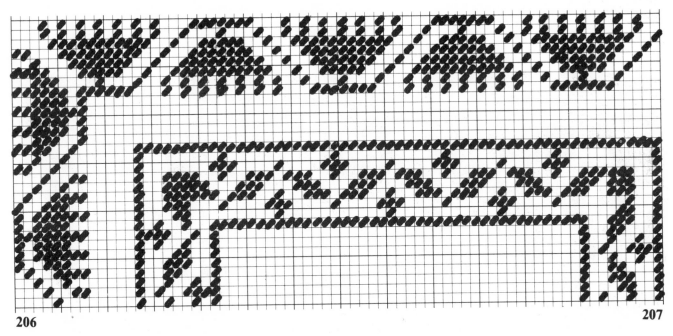

206   207

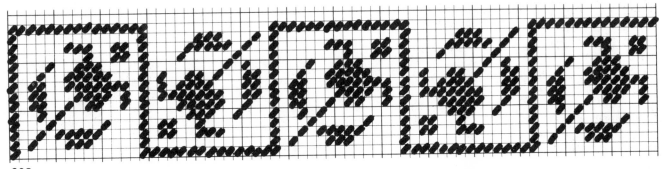

208

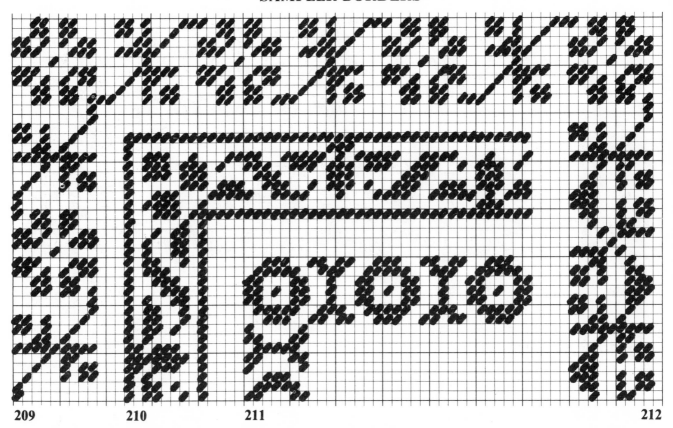

209   210   211   212

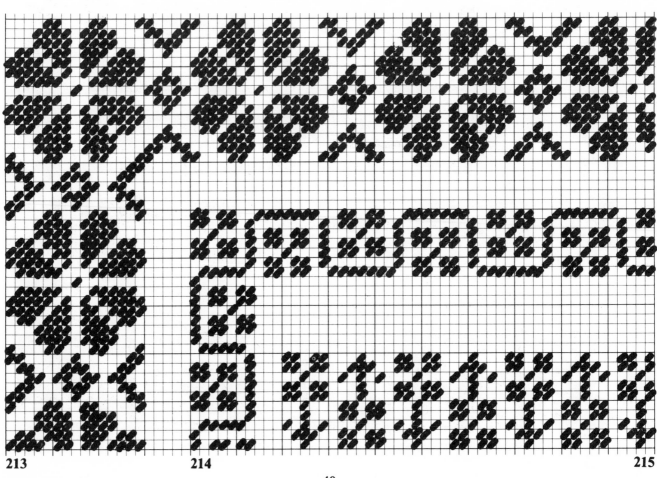

213   214   215

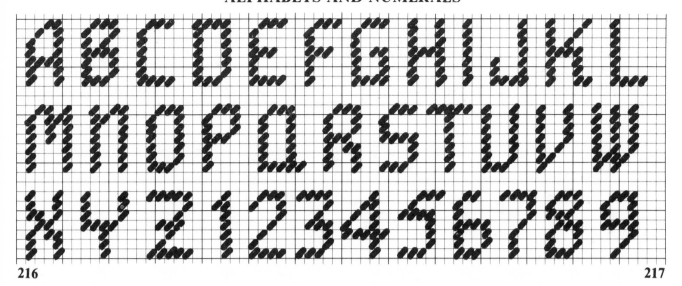

216   217

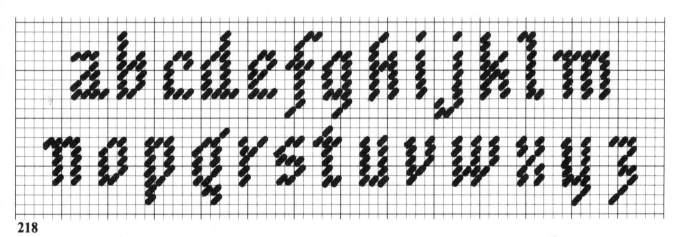

218

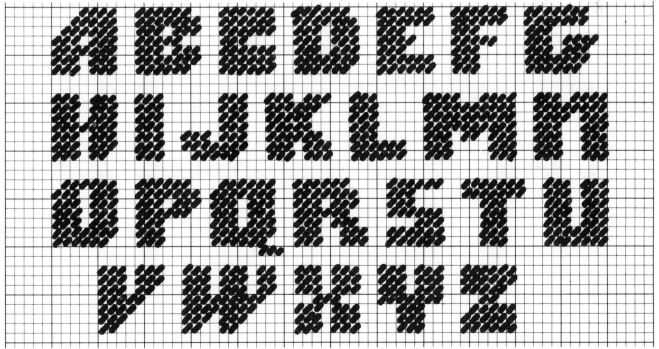

219

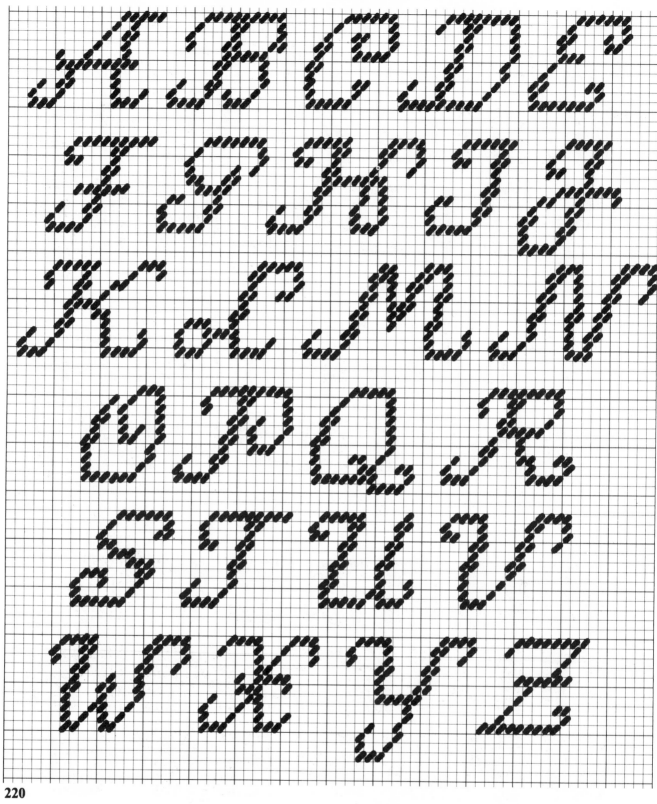

220

221

222

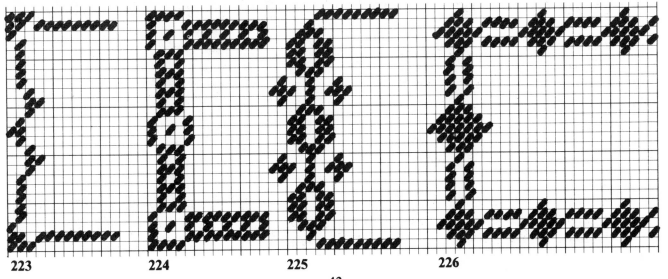

223　　224　　225　　226

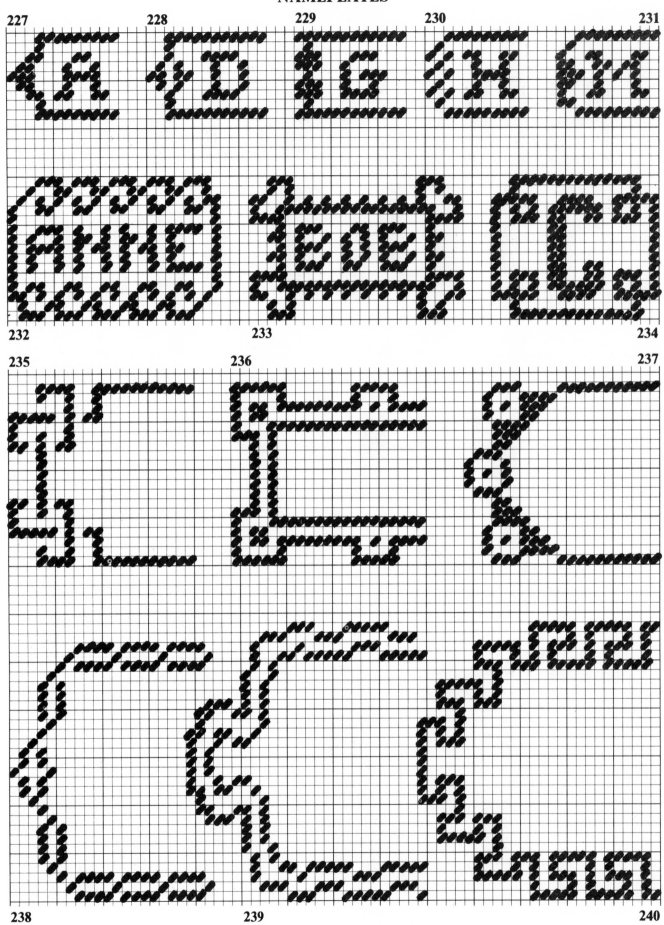

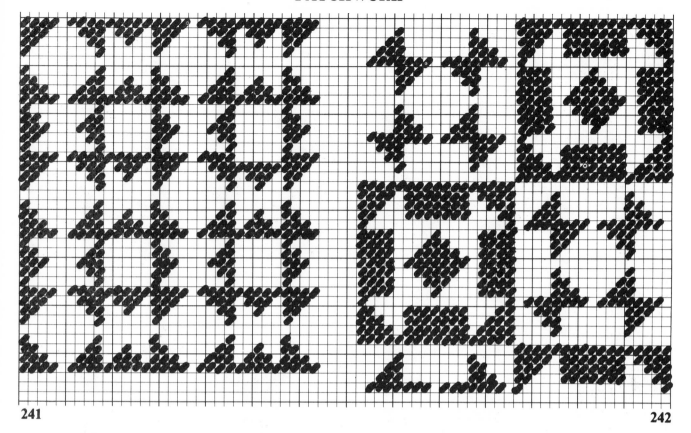

241

242

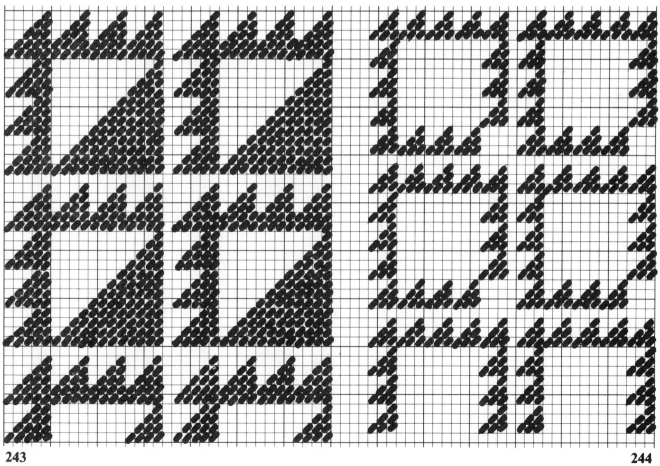

243

244

245

246

247

248

249

250

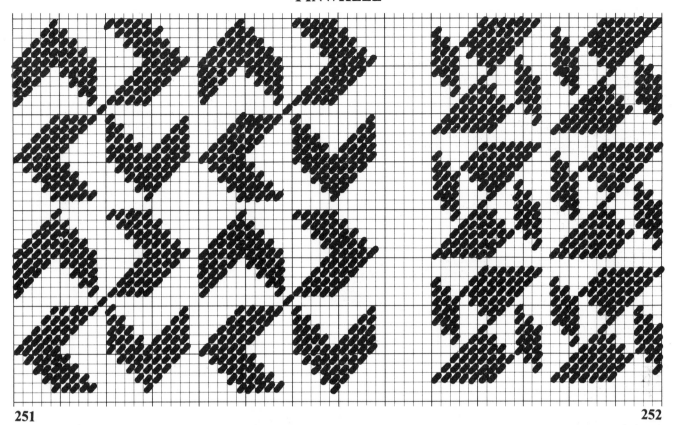

251   252

253

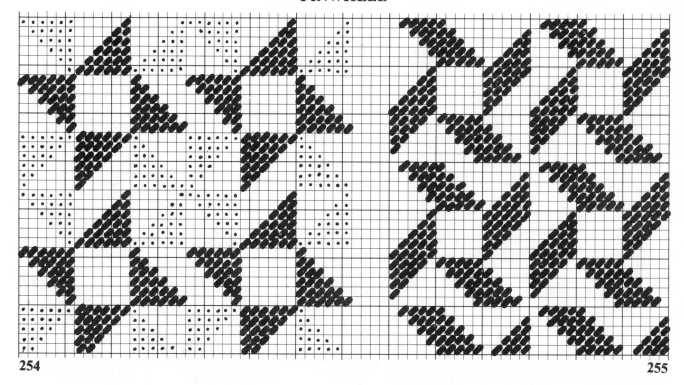

254

255

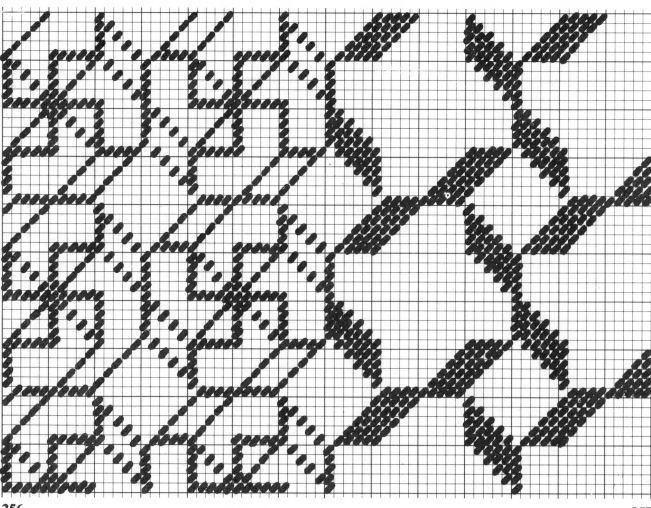

256

257

PINWHEEL

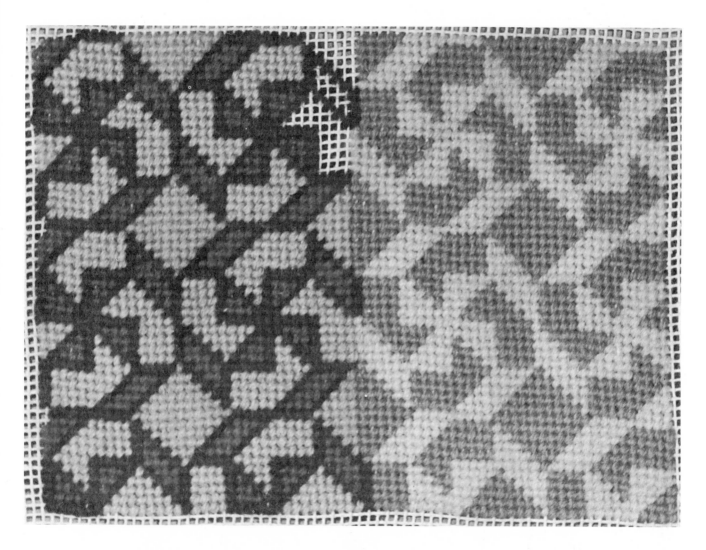

Design 256 In the left hand portion, the outlined design was filled in with bright colors. In the right hand portion, the outline color was used to fill the spaces while the background was filled in with white.

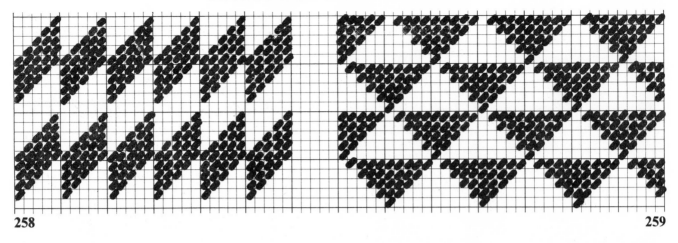

258   259

260   261

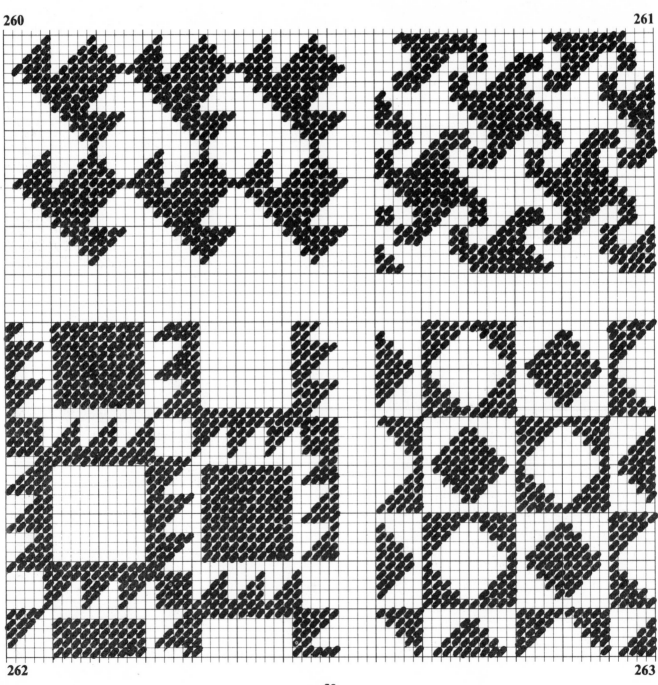

262   263

264   265

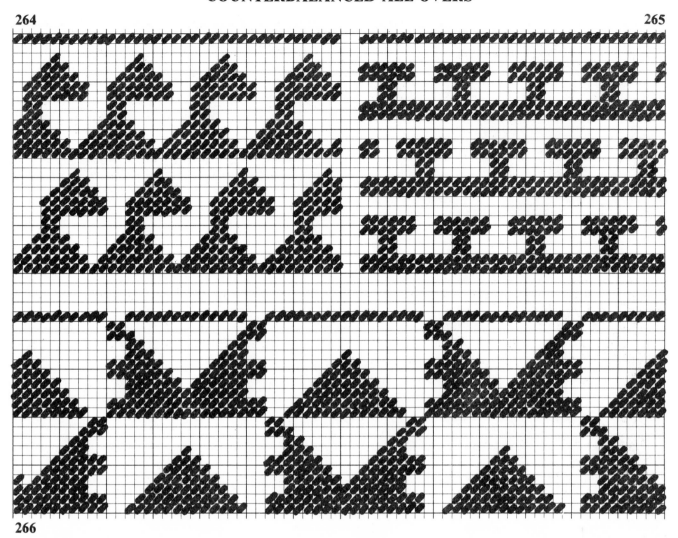

266

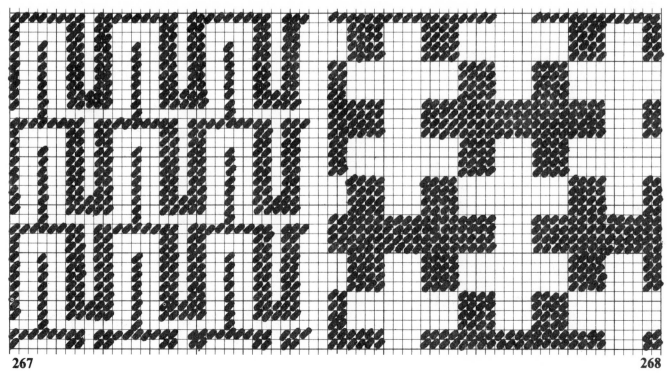

267   268

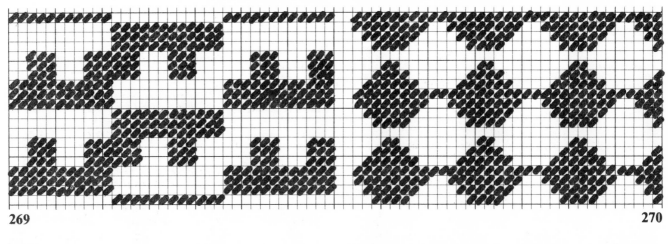

269   270

271   272

273   274

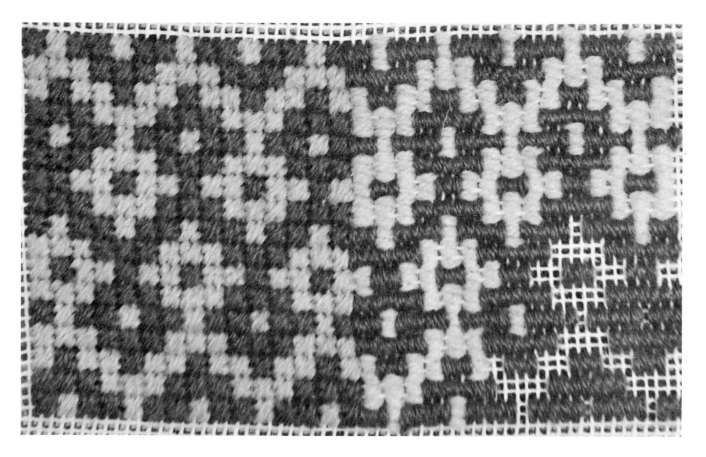

Design 271 The left hand portion was done in Mosaic Stitch. The right hand portion was done in Straight Gobelin Stitch. Two colors were used. If done in a single color, the play of light on the horizontal and vertical stitches would define the pattern.

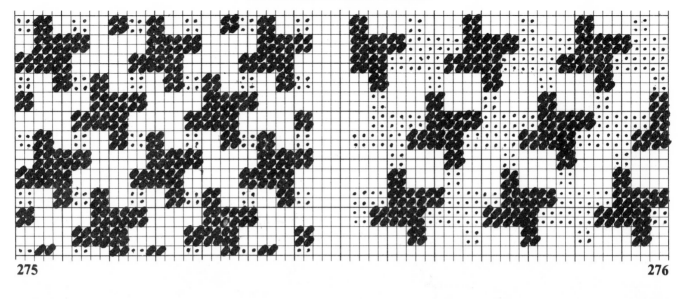

275   276

277   278

279   280

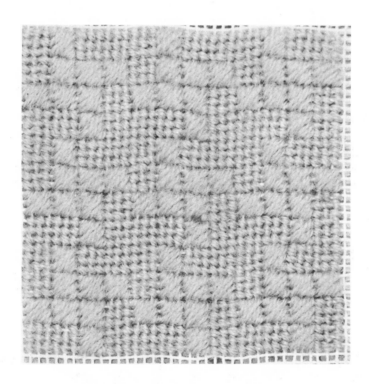

Design 277 One color was used. Delineation of pattern is achieved by contrast of texture. Counterbalanced designs are often successfully executed in this manner.

281 282
283 284
285 286
287 288
289 290
291
292

293

294

295

296

297

298

299

300

301

302

303

304

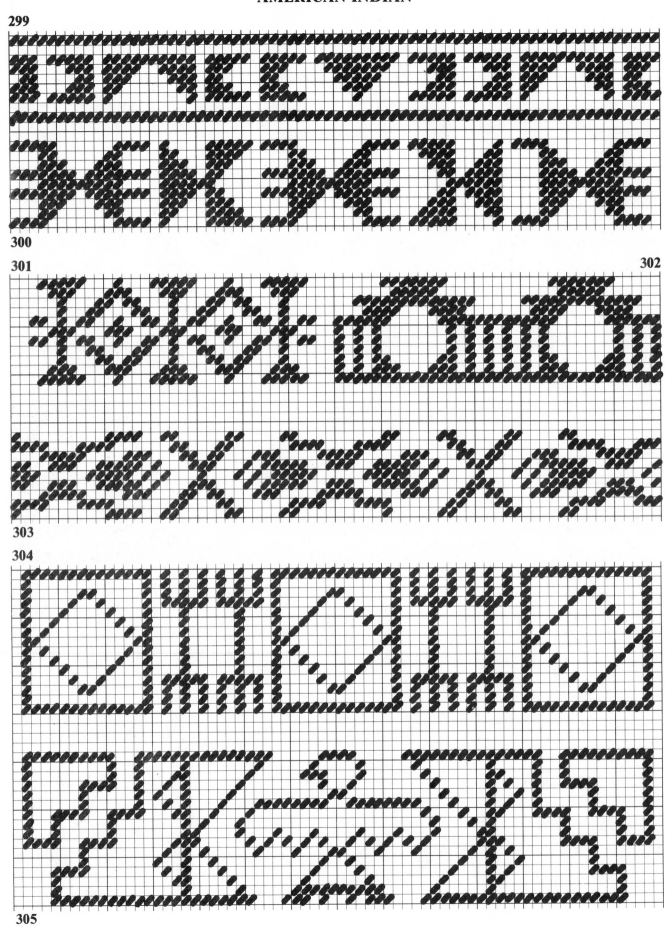

305

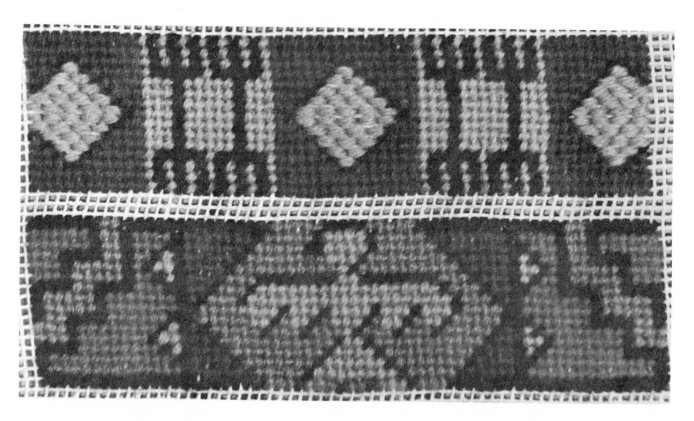

Designs 304 and 305 Outlined areas of the designs were filled in with a typical Southwestern Indian color combination—beige, rust, turquoise, and orange.

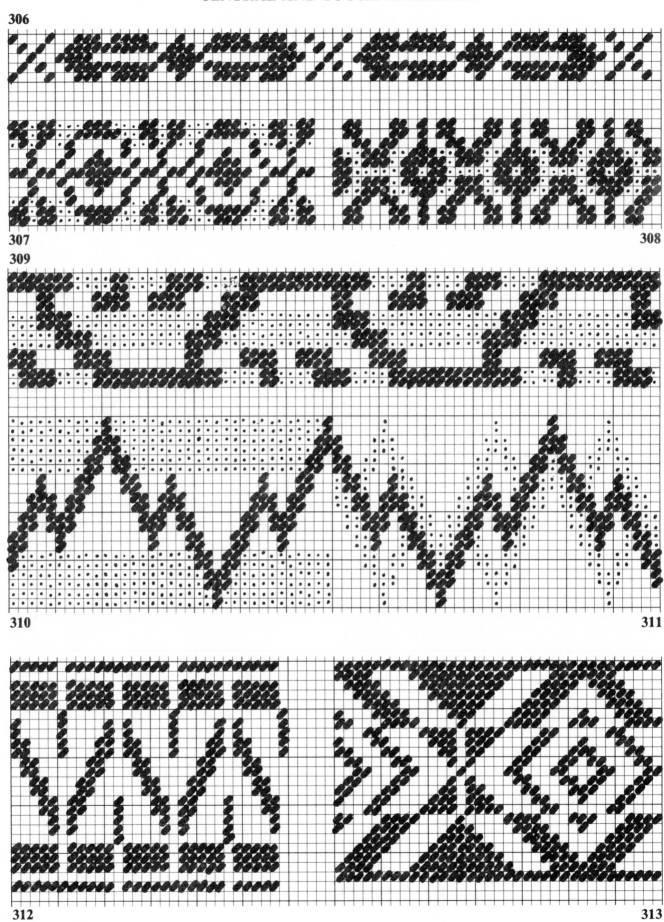

306

307   308

309

310   311

312   313

314

315

316

317

318

319

320

321

322

323

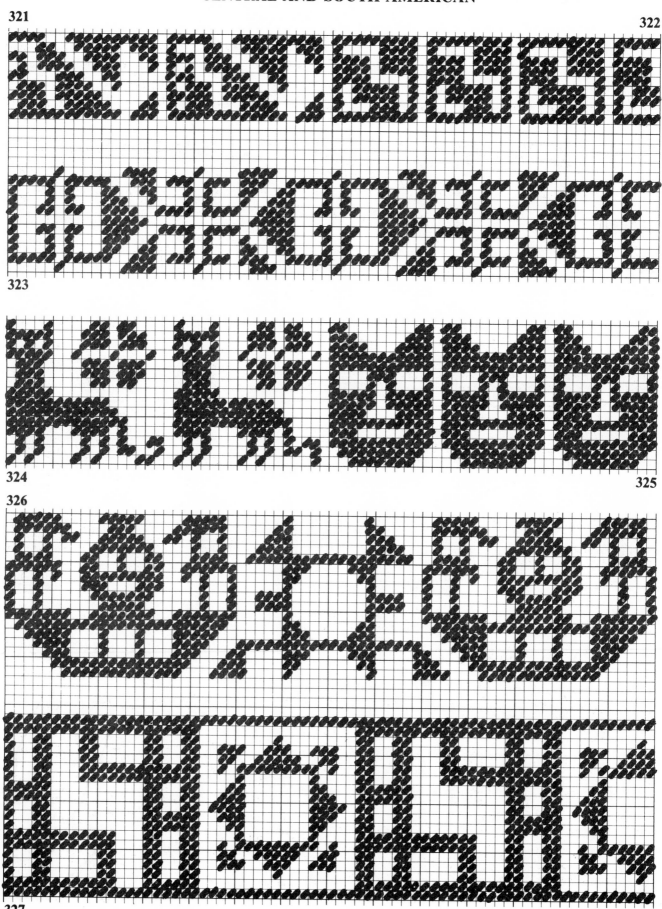

324

325

326

327

328

329

330

331

332

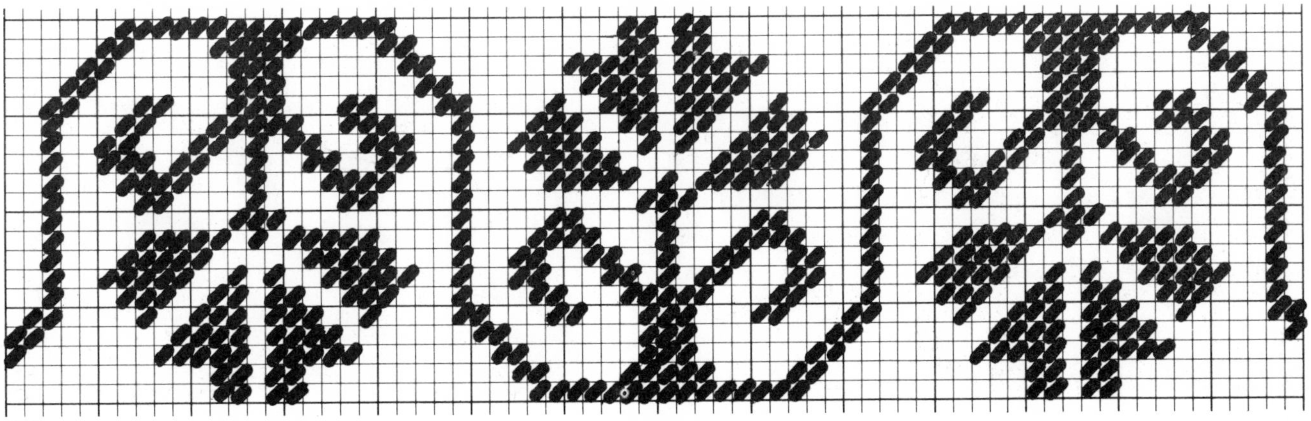

333

334

335

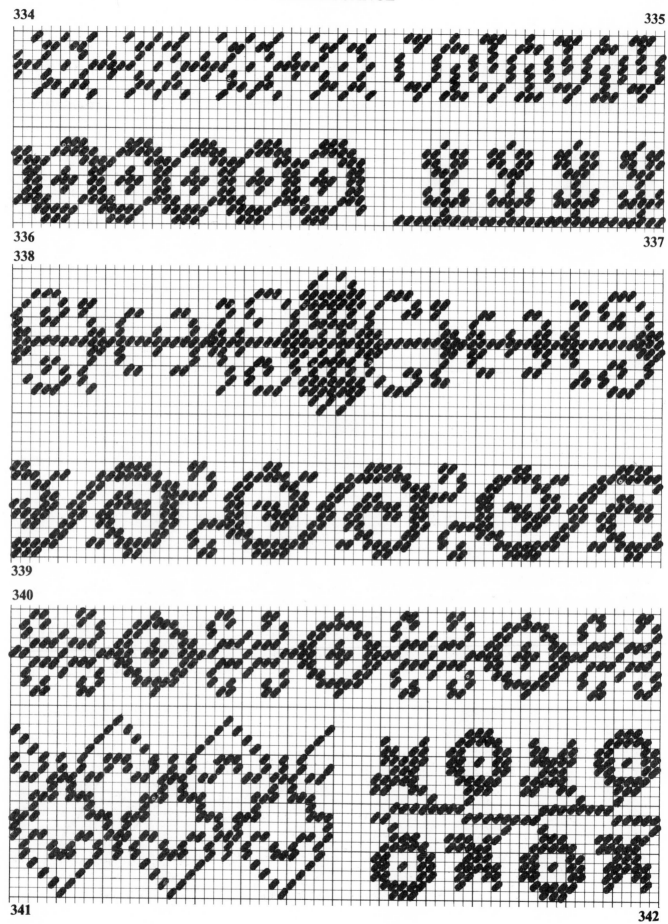

336

337

338

339

340

341

342

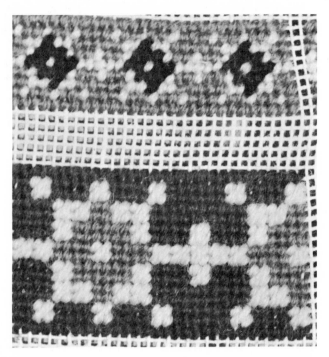

Design 334 As graphed and double scale.

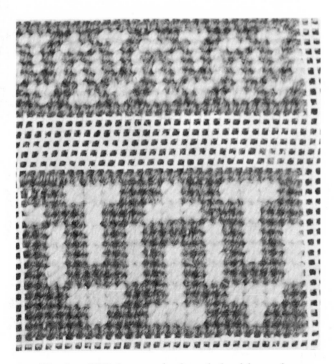

Design 335 As graphed and double scale.

An easy way to enlarge a design is to work over four stitches (as in the Mosaic Stitch) for each stitch shown in the graph.

343

344

345

346

347

348

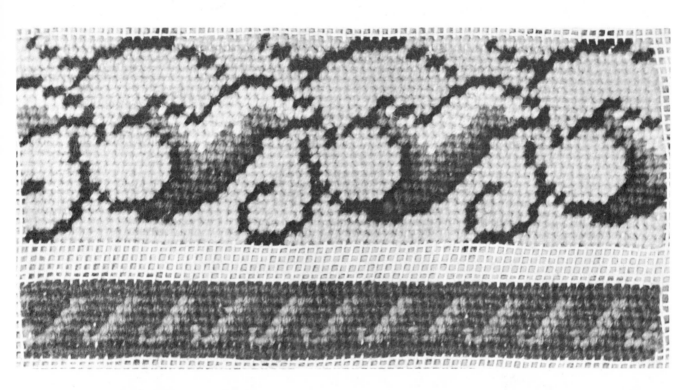

Designs 346 and 343 Where space permits, color gradations will add interest and beauty.

349

350

351

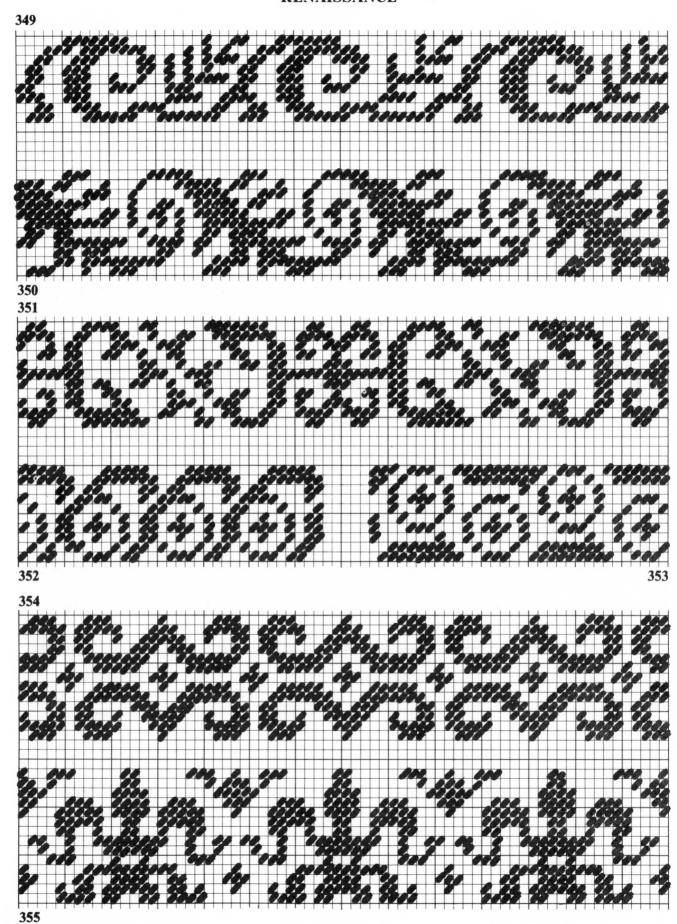

352

353

354

355

356

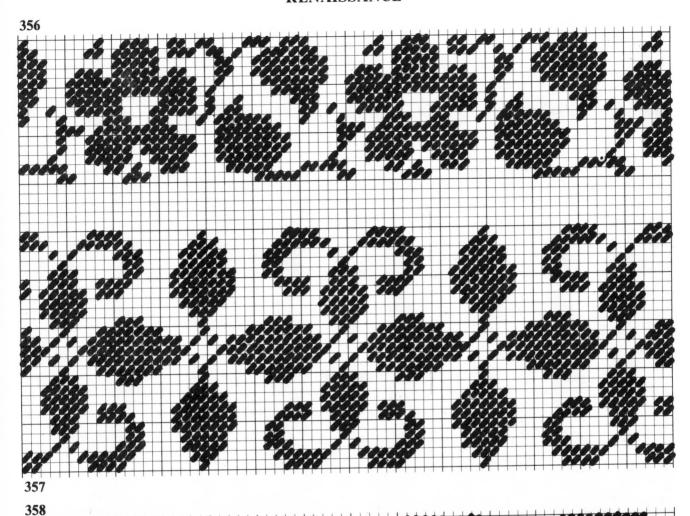

357

358

359

360

361

362

363

364

365

366

367

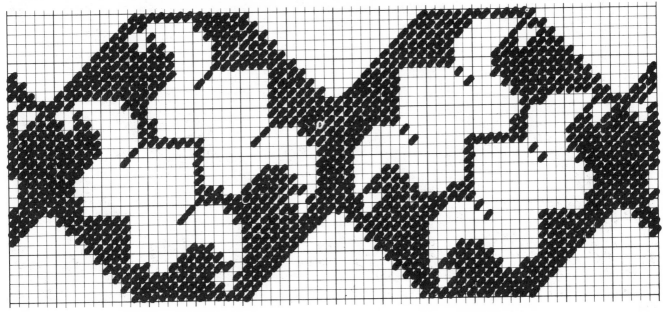

368

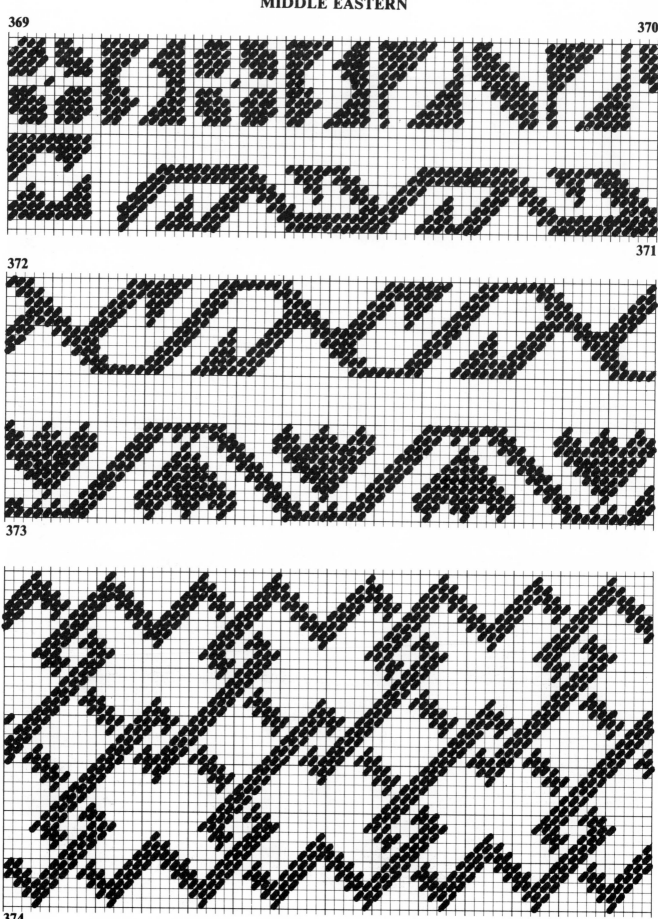

375

376

377

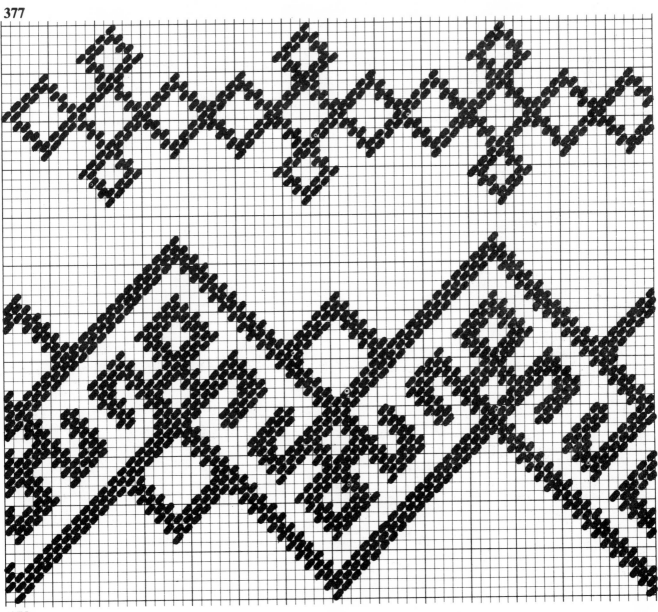

378

379

380

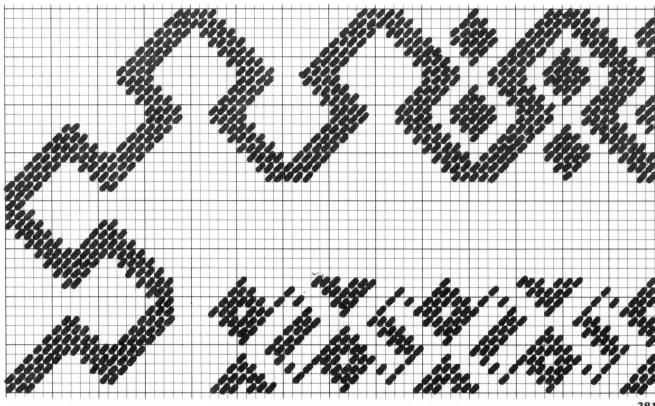

381

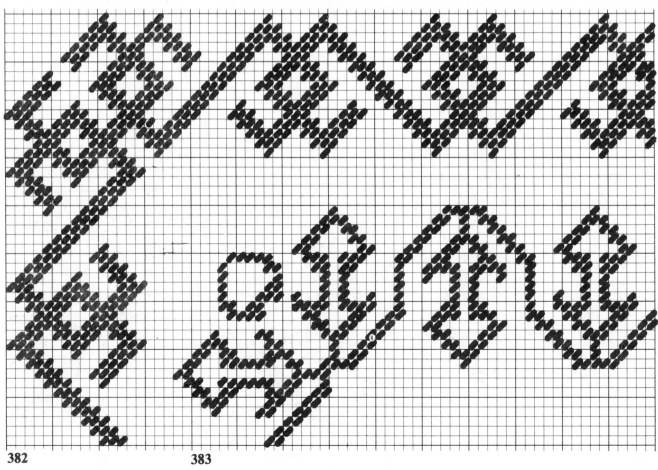

382

383

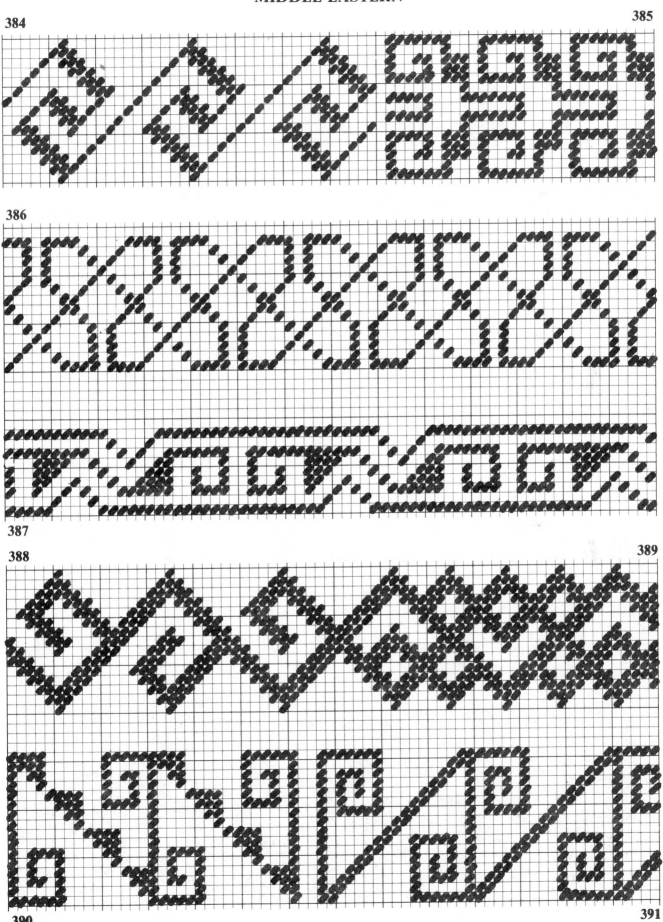

392

393

394

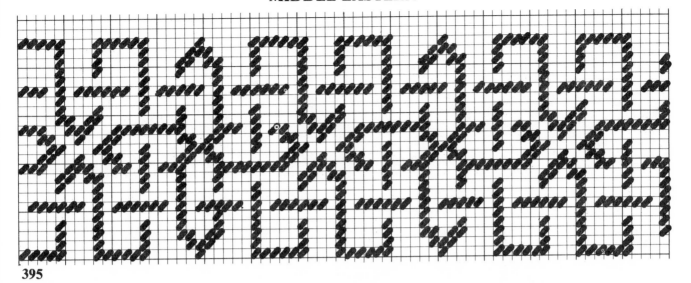

395

396

397

398

399

400

401

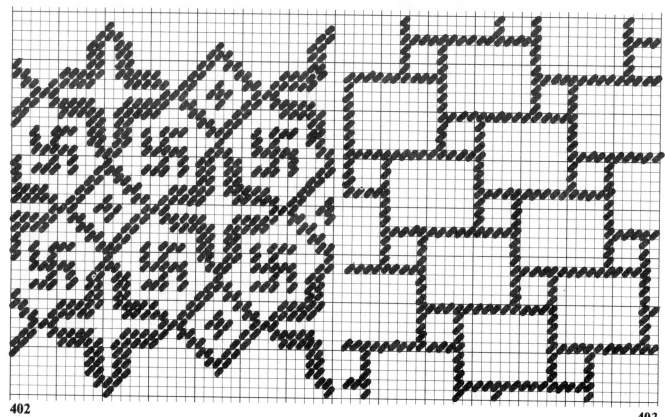

402

403

404

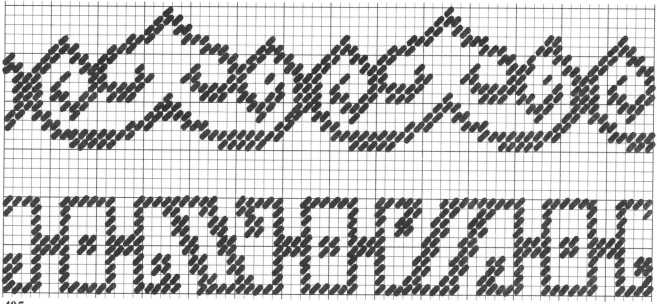

405

406

407

408

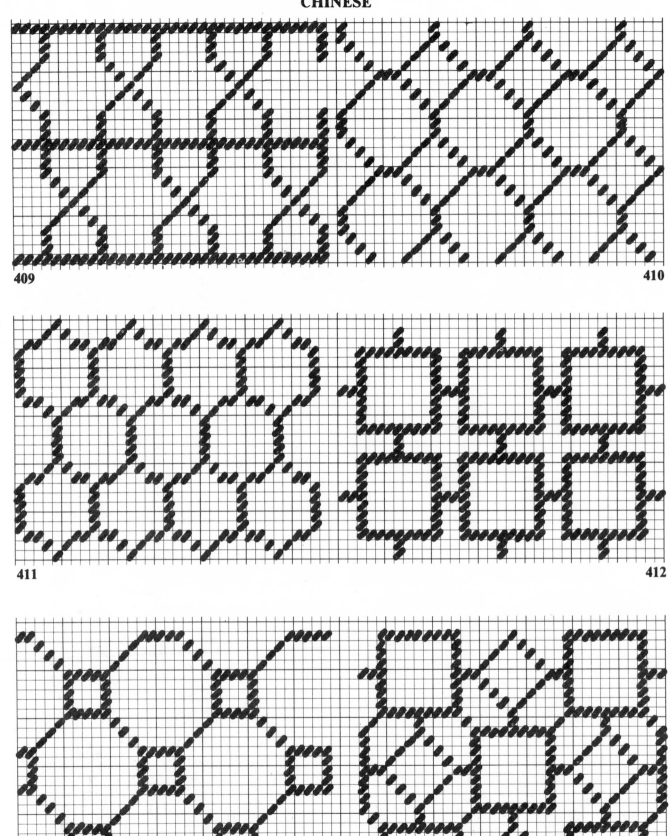

409

410

411

412

413

414

Designs 409, 410, 411, 412, 413 and 414 Pastel or monotone combinations give these patterns a soft, airy, feminine look. Use vivid colors and strong contrasts for deep, rich, more masculine effects.

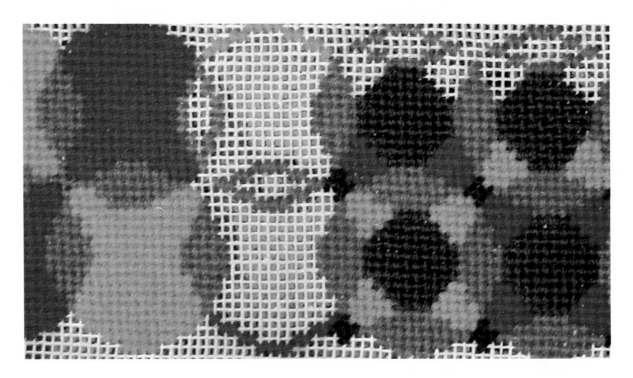

Designs 415 and 416 The same designs executed both with and without outline.

Use a dark outline to define shapes boldly. Eliminate the outline if a softer, more subtle effect is desired.

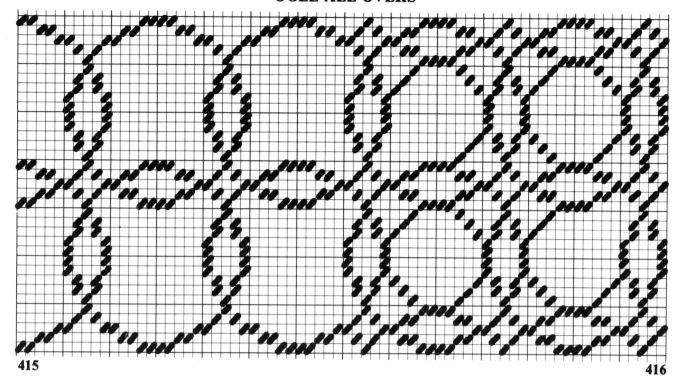

415

416

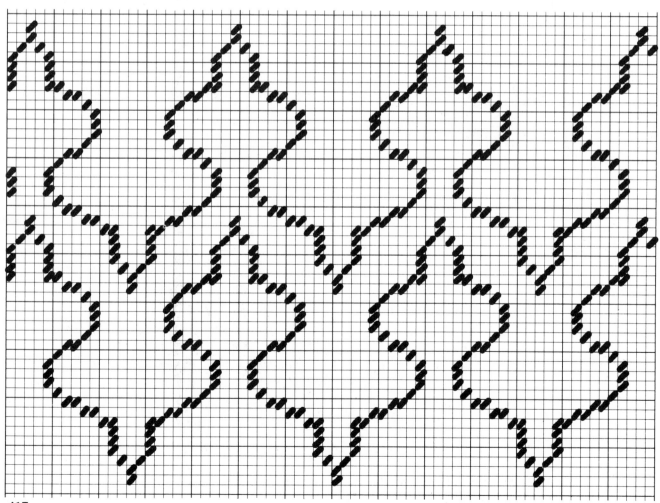

417

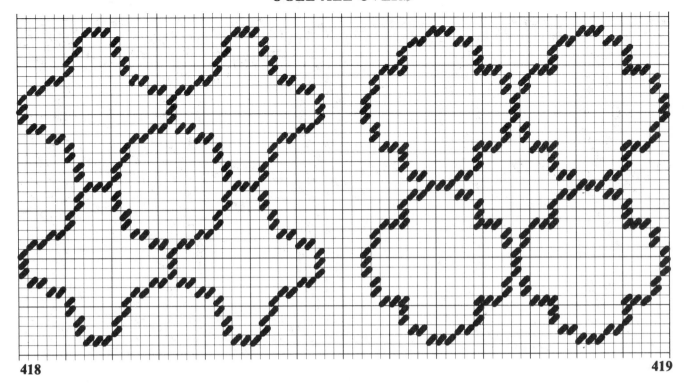

418

419

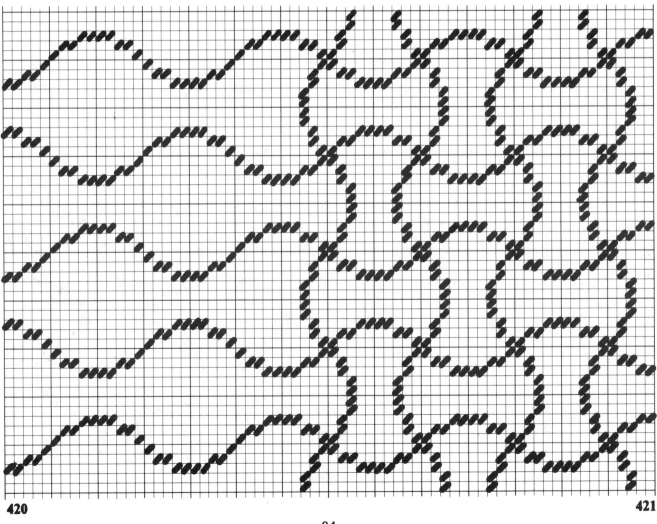

420

421

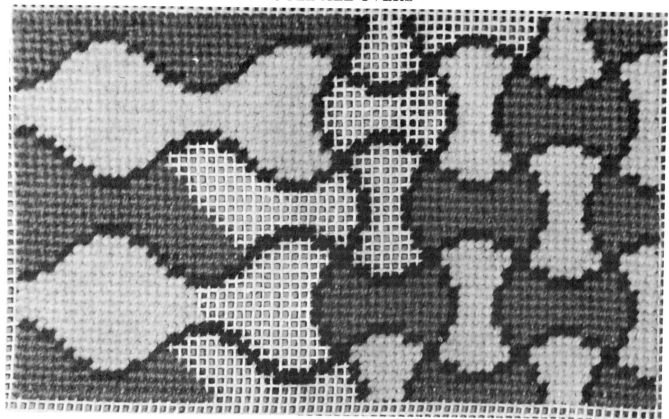

Designs 420 and 421 Here the design is outlined as graphed and two colors were used as space-fillers

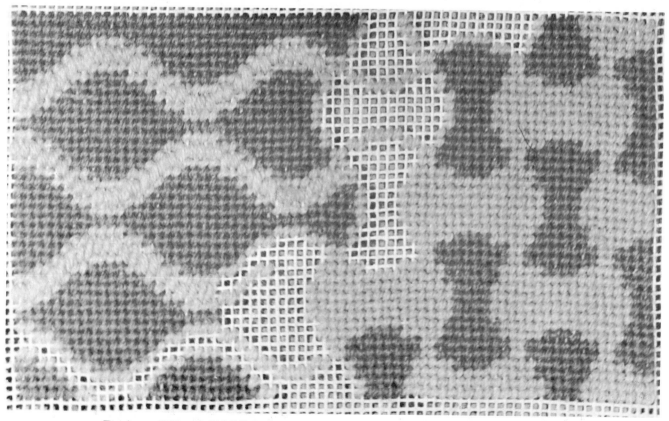

Designs 420 and 421 Liberties were taken here. The outline was broadened in the left hand portion, eliminated in the right hand portion. Only two colors were used.

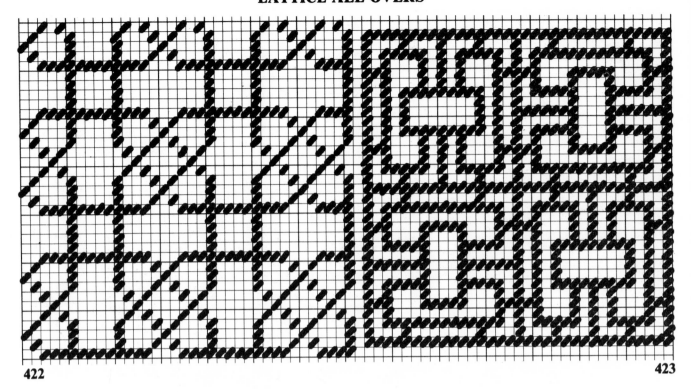

422   423

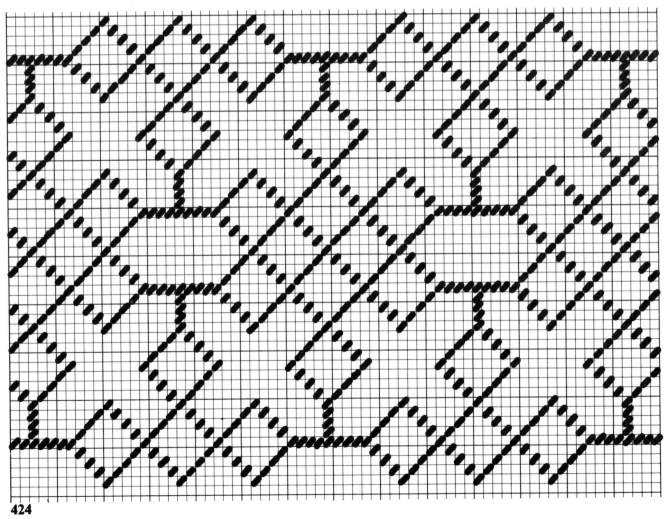

424

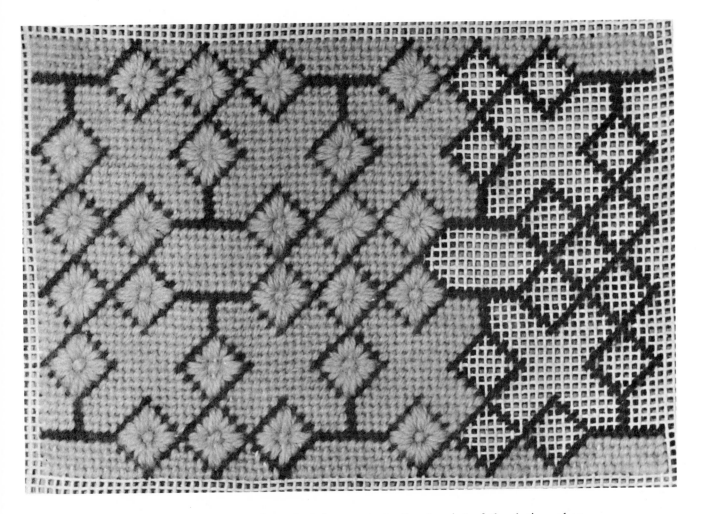

Design 424 The texturing stitch becomes the focal point of the design when done in one overall color plus an outline color.

Strong, rich colors and dark outlines would give a stained glass effect to any of the lattice designs.

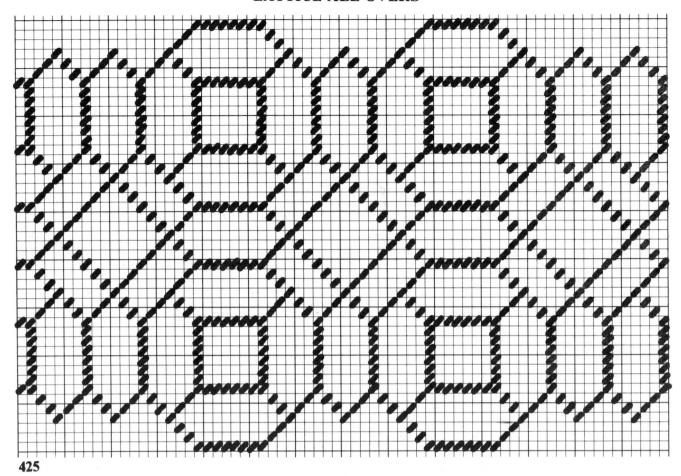

425

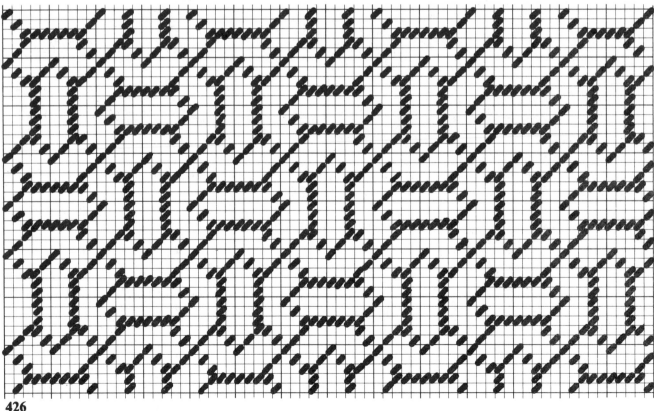

426

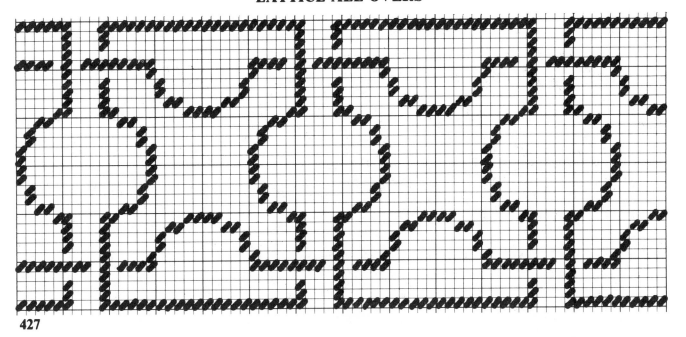

427

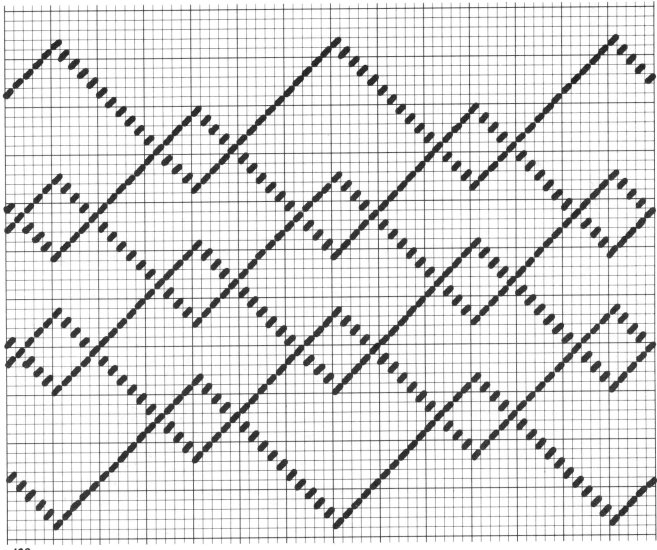

428

429

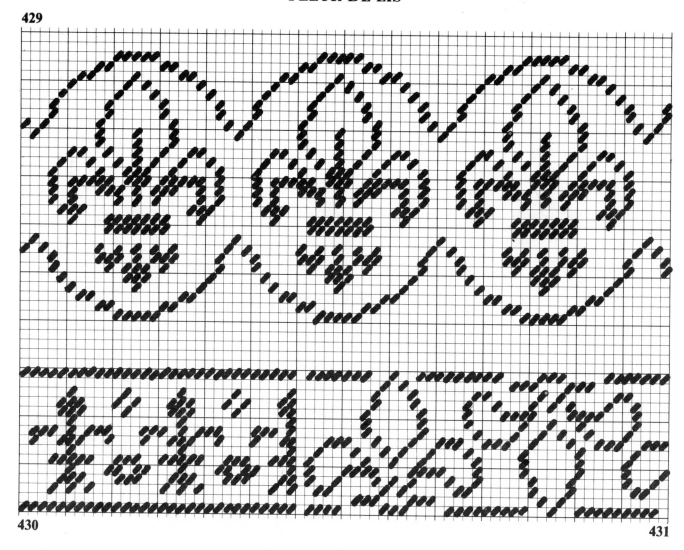

430

431

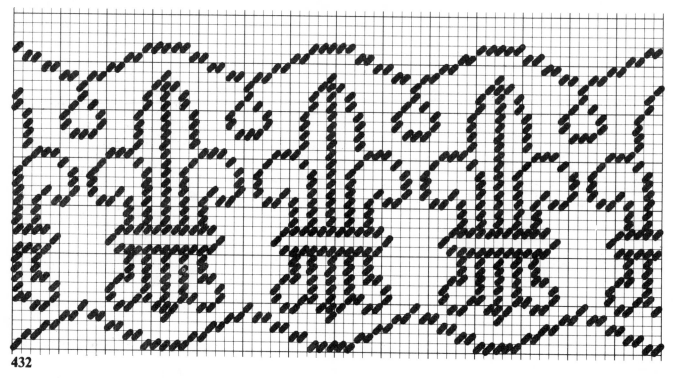

432

433

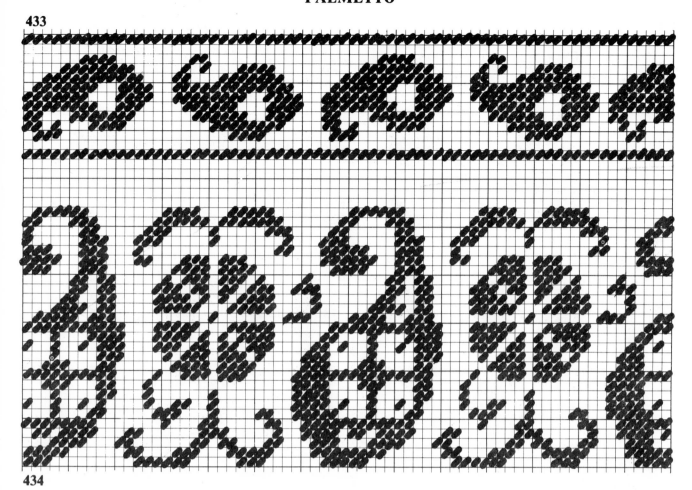

434

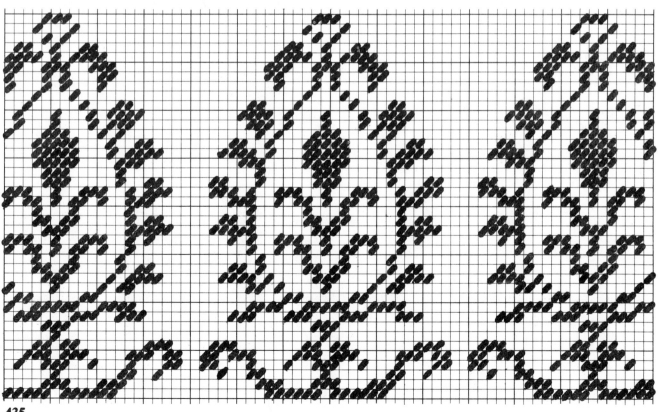

435

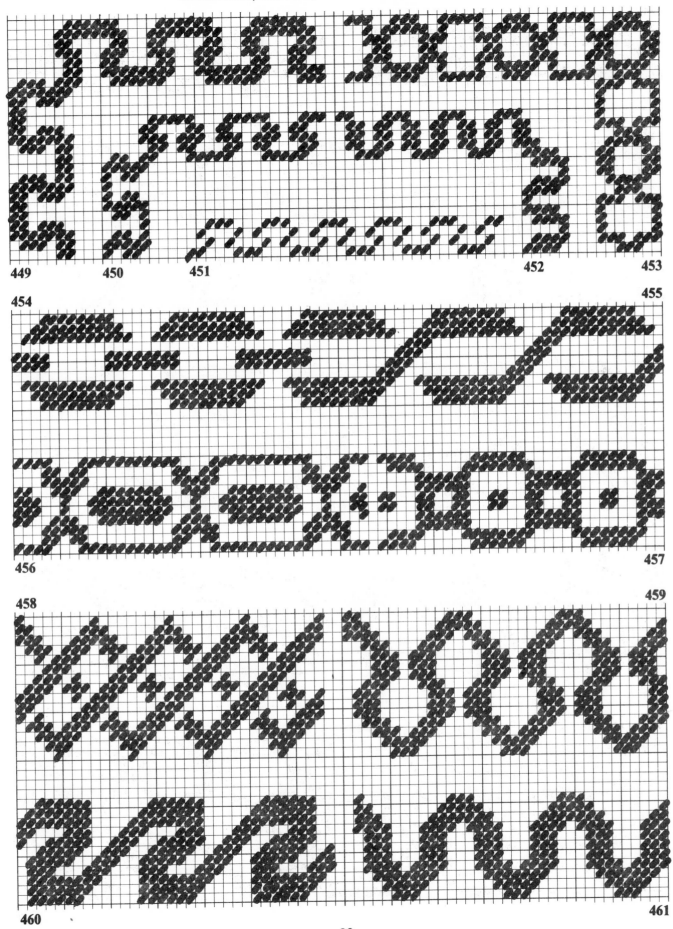

449   450   451   452   453

454   455

456   457

458   459

460   461

462

463

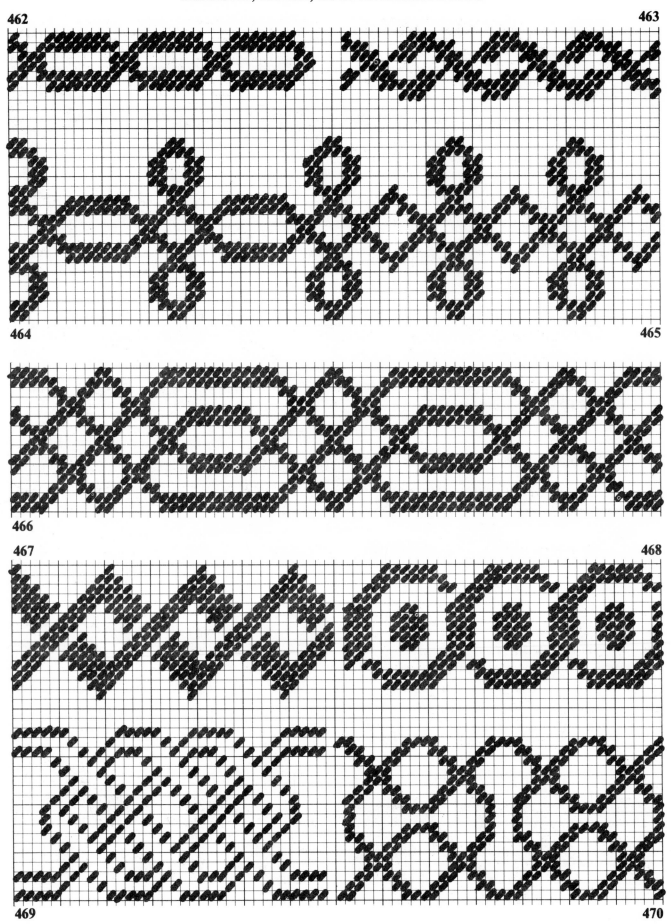

464

465

466

467

468

469

470

471

472

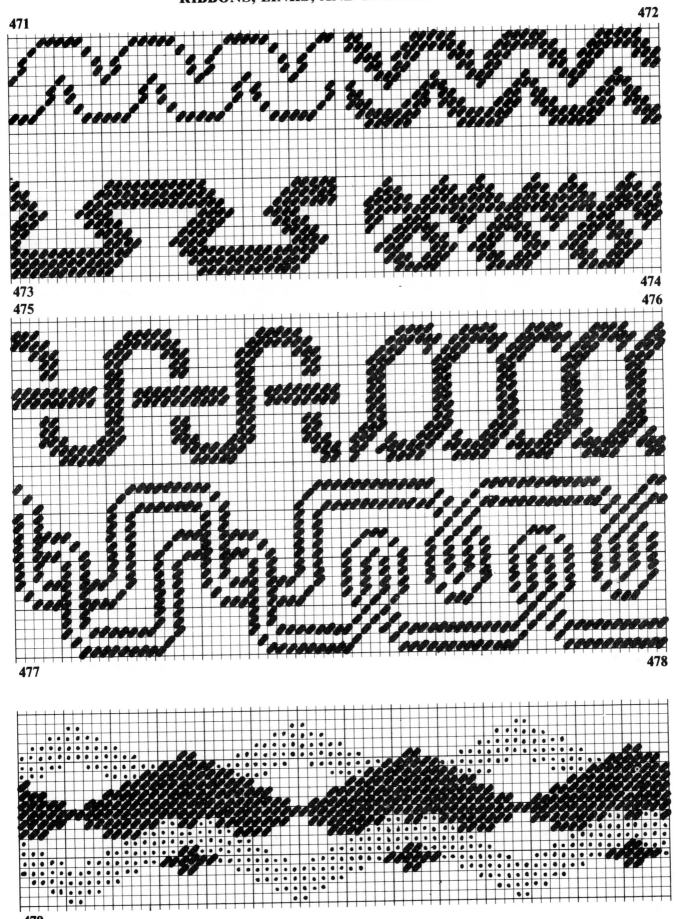

473

474

475

476

477

478

479

480

481

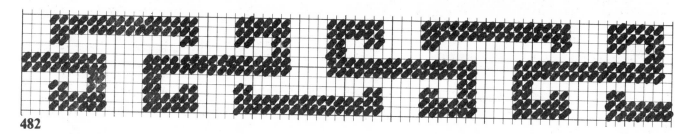

482

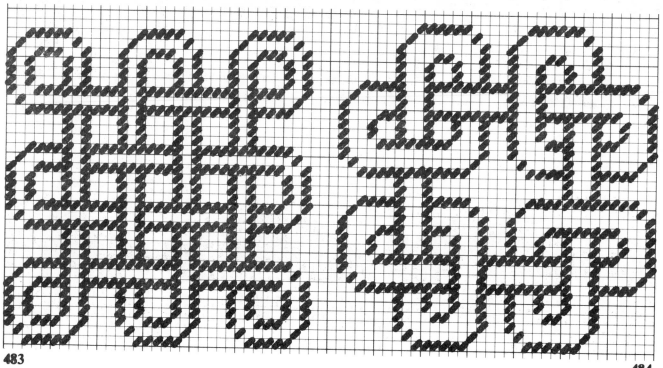

483

484

485   486   487   488

489

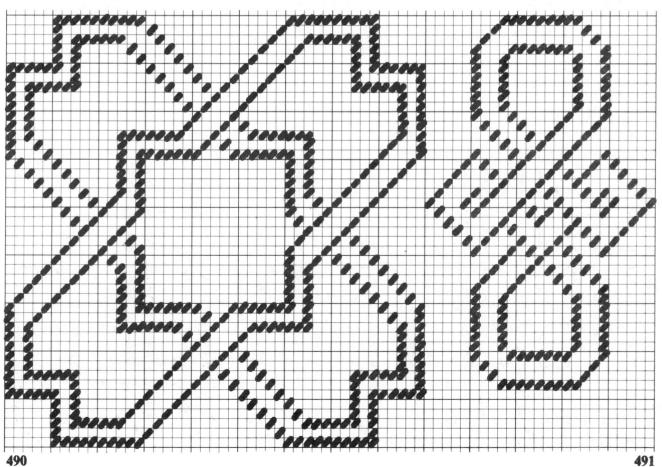

490   491

492

493 **494**

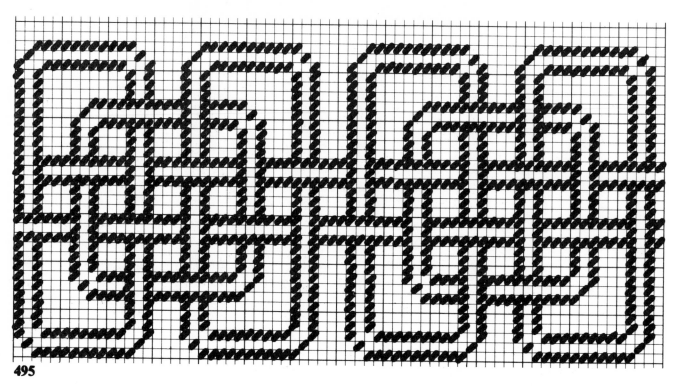

495

Design 494 This piece matches the graph exactly, with "gates" or separations to give the over-under effect of interlacing.

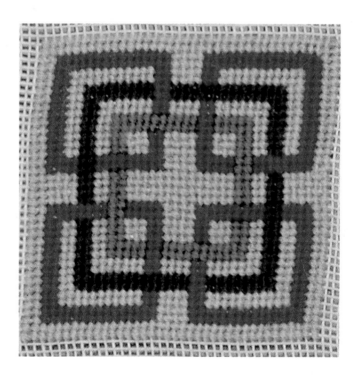

Design 494 When using several colors, the "gates" are eliminated, since the over-under sequence is maintained by color contrast.

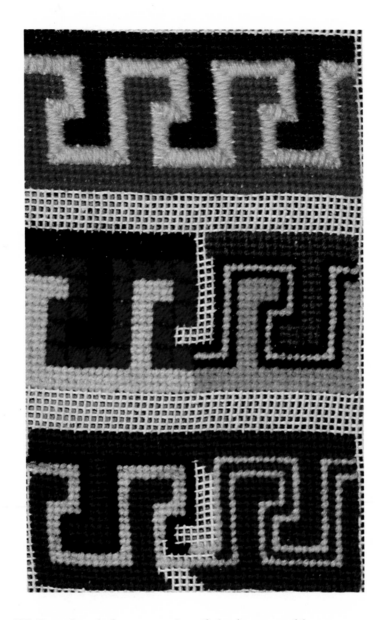

Design 498 Sampler: A few examples of the innumerable ways to execute a Greek Key design.

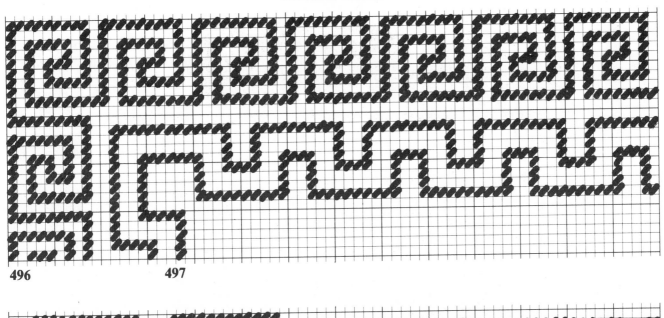

496   497

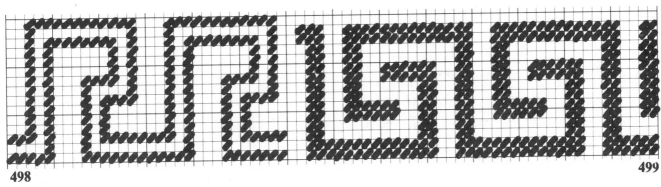

498   499

500   501

502   503

504

505

506

507

508

509

510

511

512

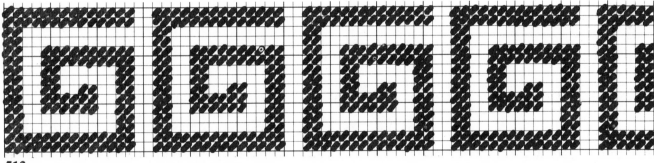

513
514

515

Design 525 This horizontal band with motif in a diagonal position from upper left to lower right is like the chart on the opposite page.

Any horizontal design may be converted to a vertical design by either of the two methods shown.

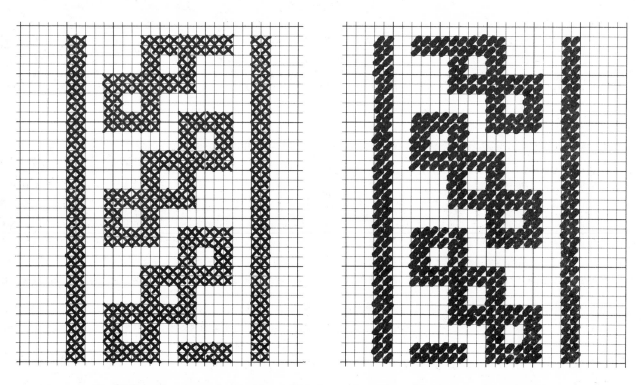

(Left) Graph was copied in Cross Stitch symbol, then the copy was turned 90°. An incorrect angle of the Half-Cross Stitch symbol will no longer be a source of confusion when working in Tent Stitch.

(Right) Preferred method: This graph is an exact copy of graphed design 525 as seen reversed in a mirror held along top or upper edge. Copy was then turned 90°.

516 517   518

519   520

521   522

523

524   525

526   527   528   529

530   531   532

533   534

535

SAMPLE GRID

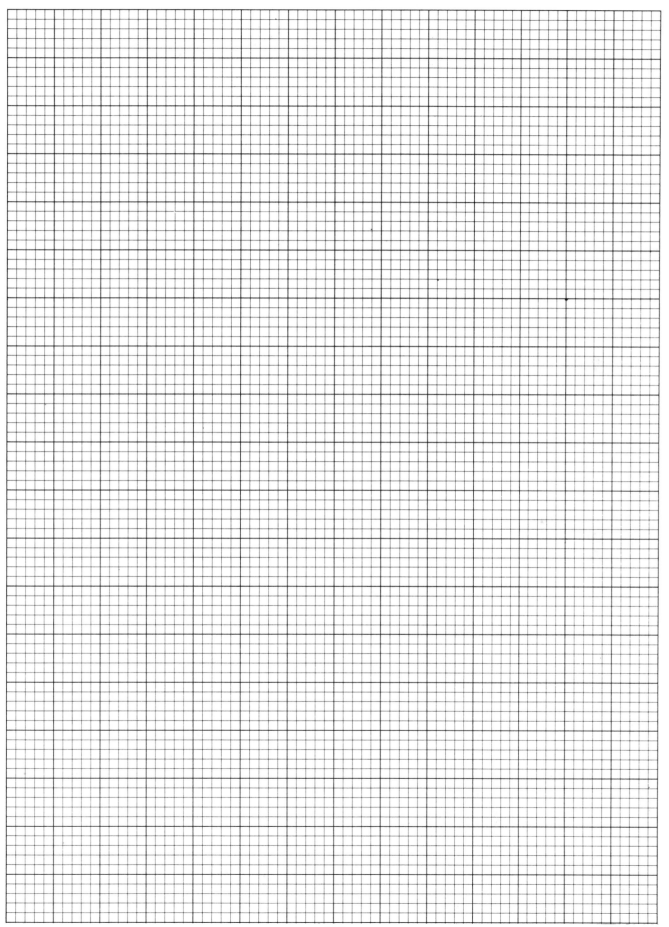

II
Cross Stitch

Cross Stitch Embroidery is usually associated with embroidery floss and fabrics for clothing and household linens rather than with canvas and woolen yarn, but your use of any of the one thousand and one designs in this volume need not be influenced by the graphing symbol. Only your sense of style and suitability should be the judge. So feel free to use these Cross Stitch designs for needlepoint, if you so choose.

To execute in Cross Stitch over canvas, use the design as graphed. To execute the design in Tent Stitch, however, you must regraph it in Half-Cross Stitch symbol for the reasons explained in the Section I Introduction.

Bands and borders shown in Cross Stitch symbol may be executed either horizontally or vertically in Cross Stitch without changing the graph.

Many of the designs in both sections may be used as knitting patterns or to decorate knitted or crocheted (Afghan Stitch) grounds, as shown by several of the photographs. Other illustrations demonstrate the use of Cross Stitch designs to embroider fabric in other ways, such as the transfer method or over canvas.

No one is limiting you to using these designs in the obvious or illustrated ways or in just the crafts mentioned. You may find them helpful for beading or weaving, for Black Work, Holbein, Hardanger or Guipure d'Art embroidery, just to name a few likely crafts. Use the designs in any way your fancy dictates to bring more pleasure, individuality, and diversity to your craftsmanship.

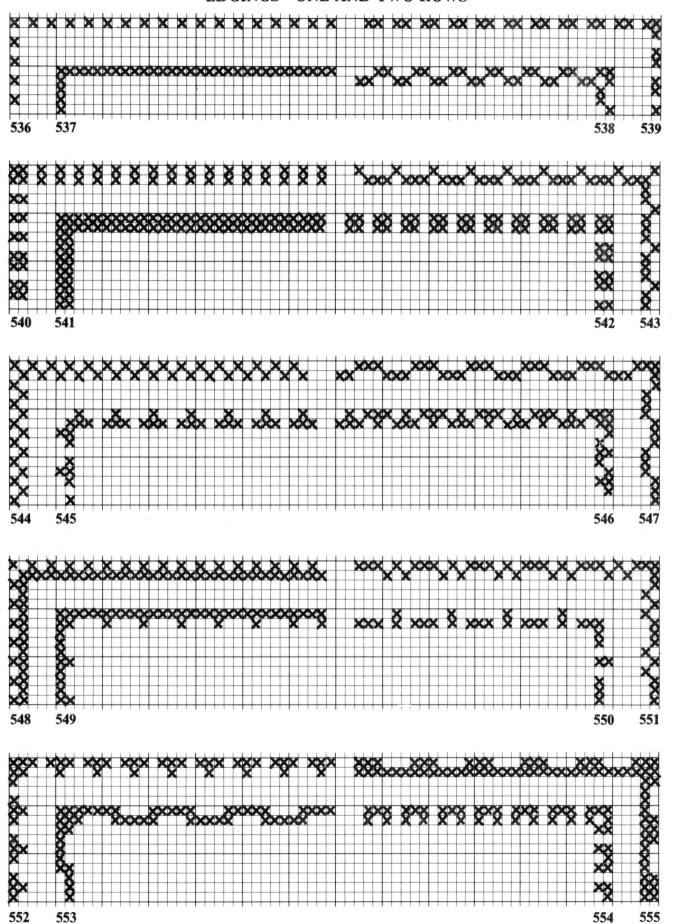

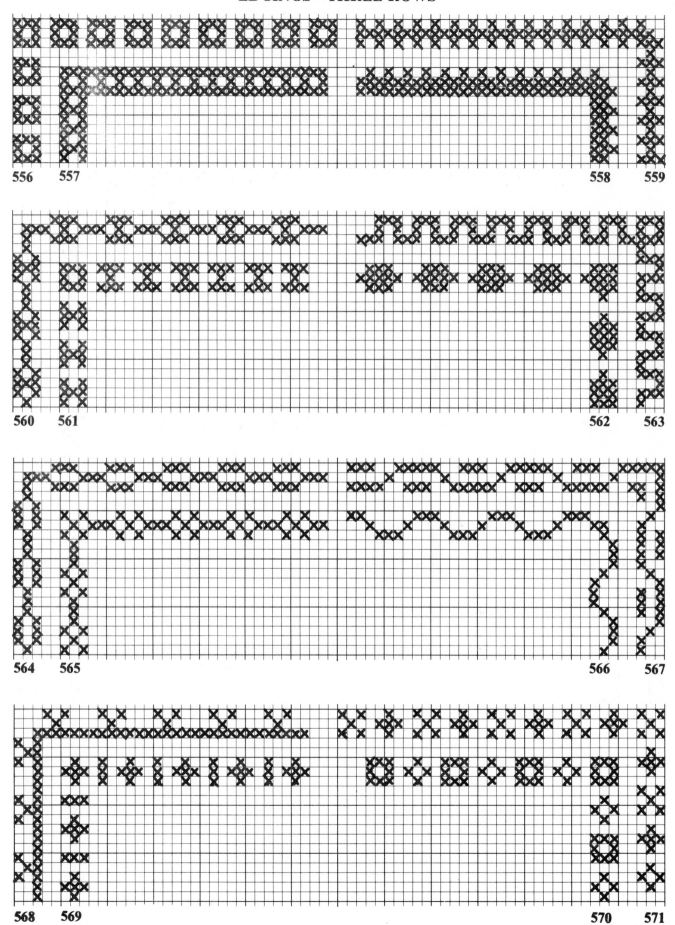

556   557   558   559

560   561   562   563

564   565   566   567

568   569   570   571

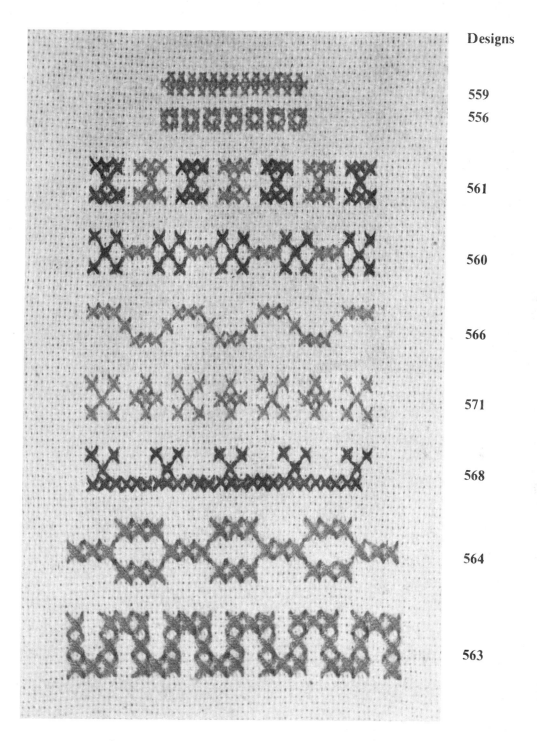

Designs

559
556

561

560

566

571

568

564

563

Comparison sampler: one, two, and three thread count.

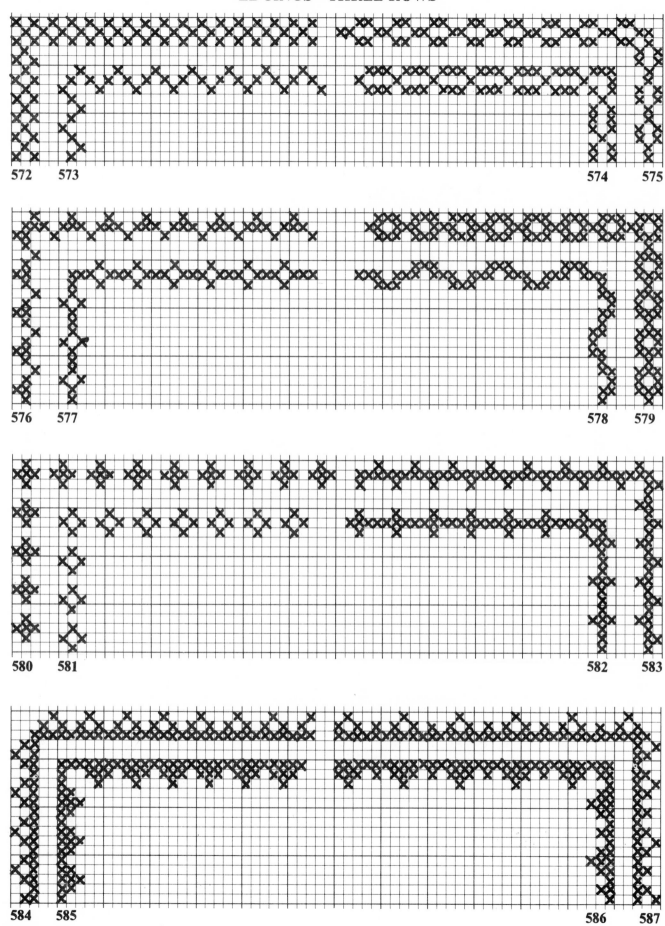

572   573   574   575

576   577   578   579

580   581   582   583

584   585   586   587

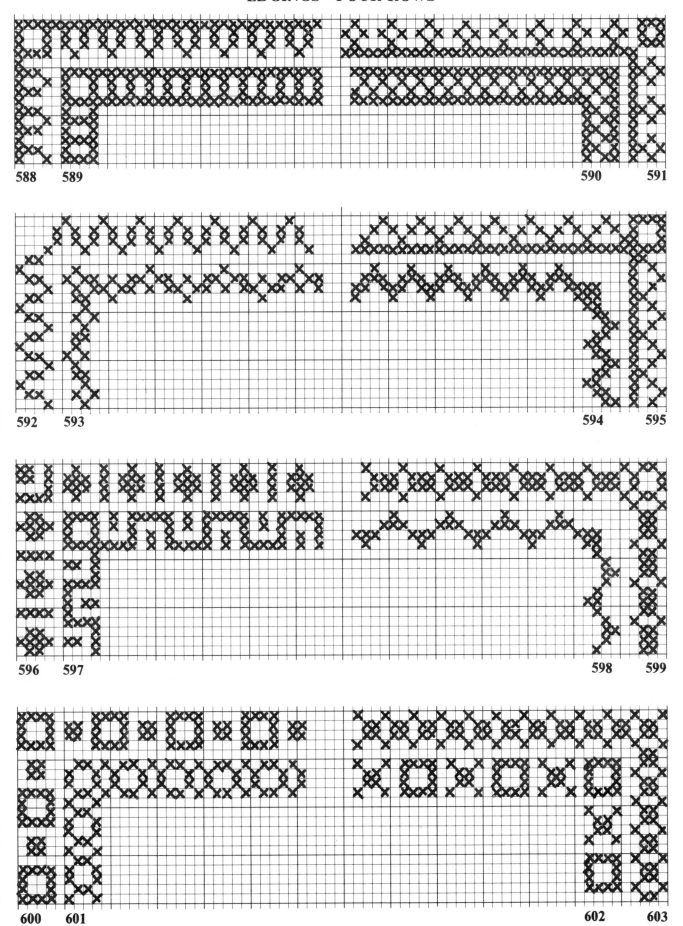

588 589   590   591

592 593   594   595

596 597   598   599

600 601   602   603

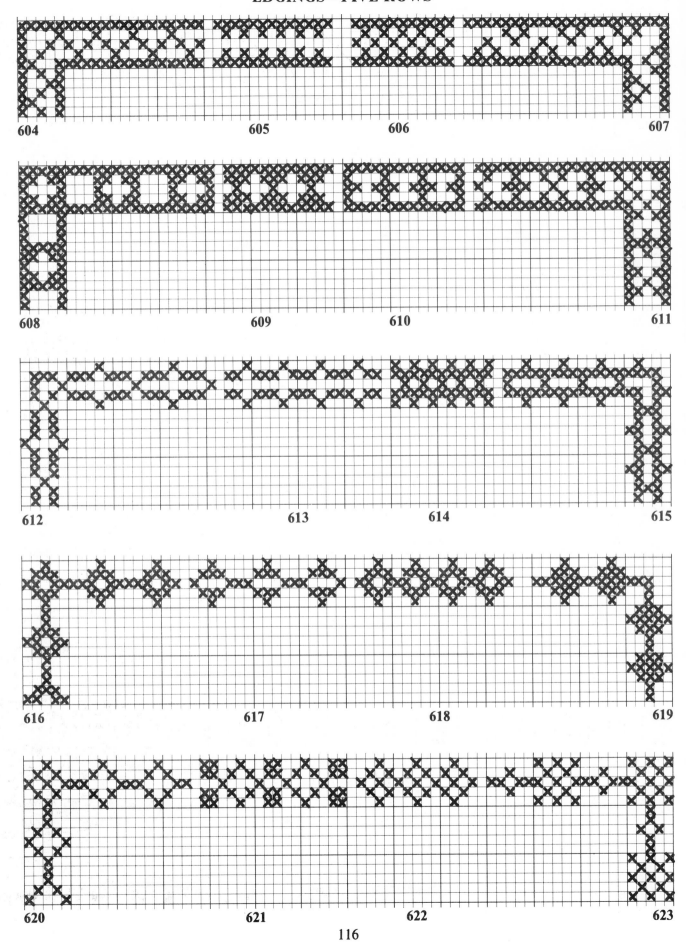

604   605   606   607

608   609   610   611

612   613   614   615

616   617   618   619

620   621   622   623

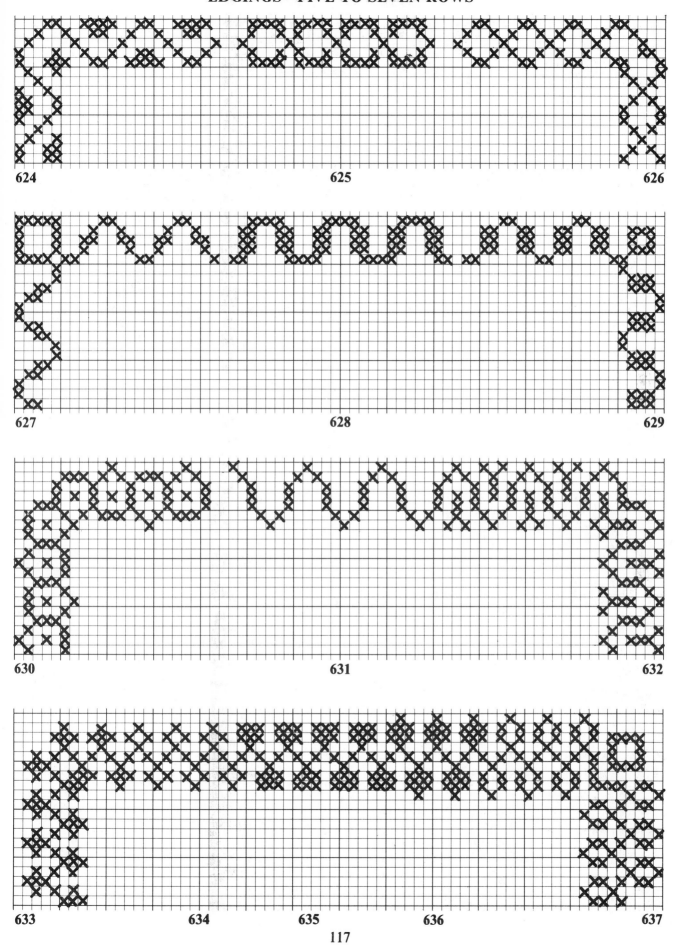

624   625   626

627   628   629

630   631   632

633   634   635   636   637

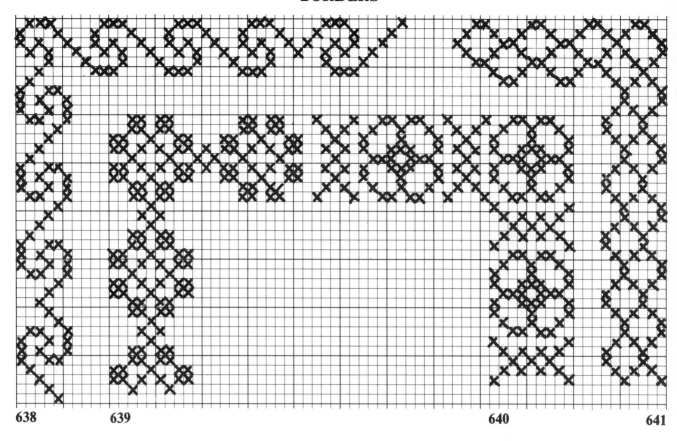

638   639   640   641

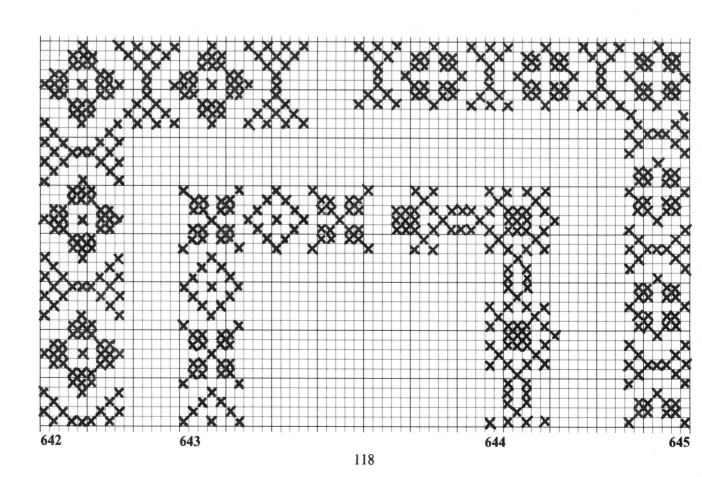

642   643   644   645

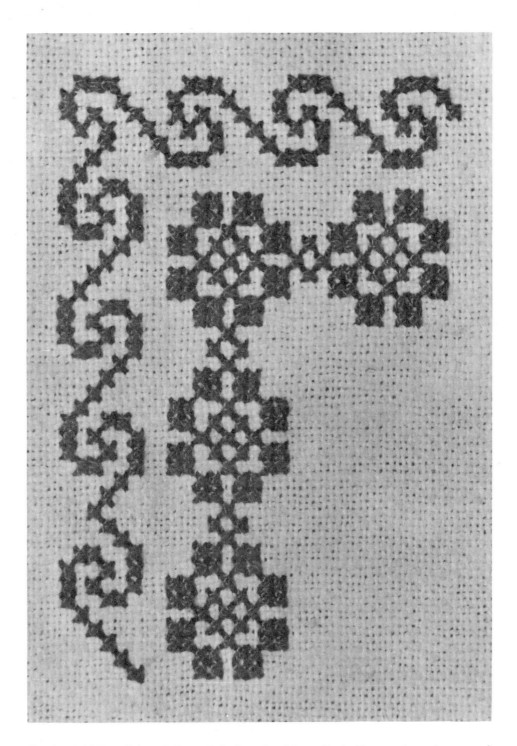

Design 638 Traditional Cross Stitch embroidery. Perle Cotton thread was used for two thread count stitch on coarse linen fabric.

646

647

648

649

650

651

652

653

654

655

656

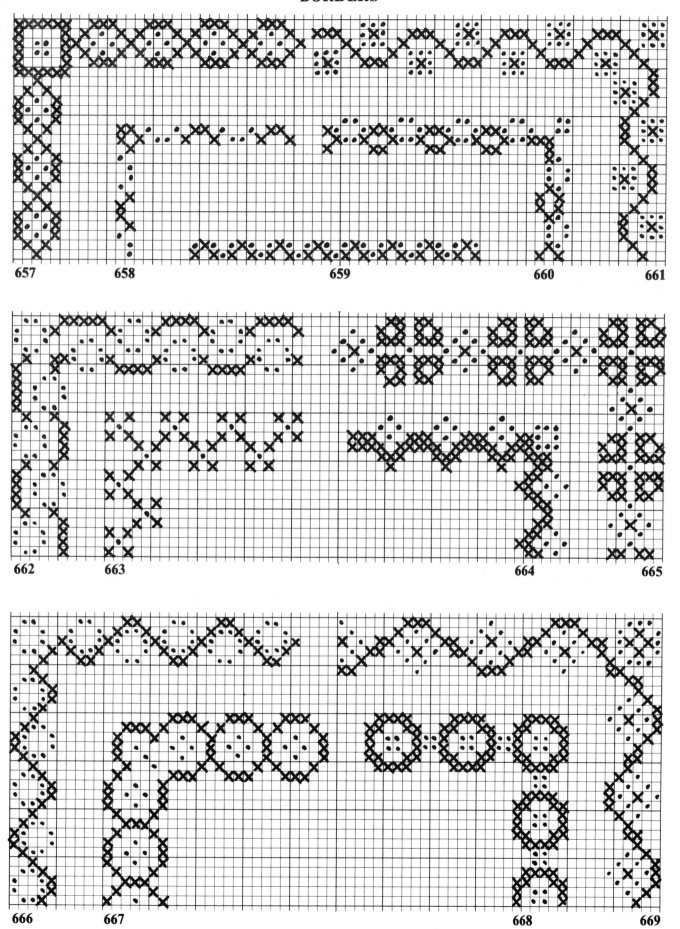

657   658   659   660   661

662   663   664   665

666   667   668   669

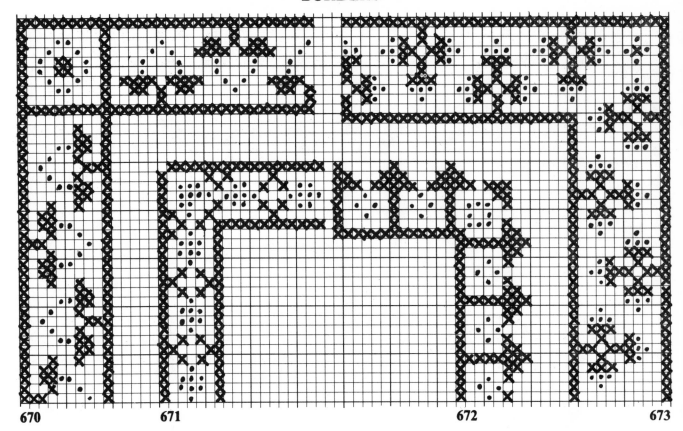

670   671   672   673

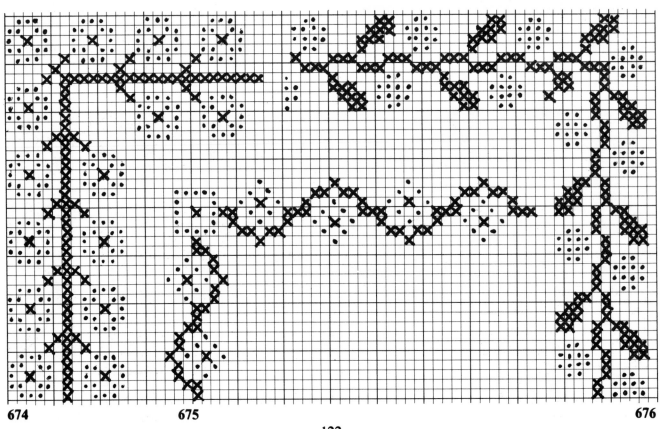

674   675   676

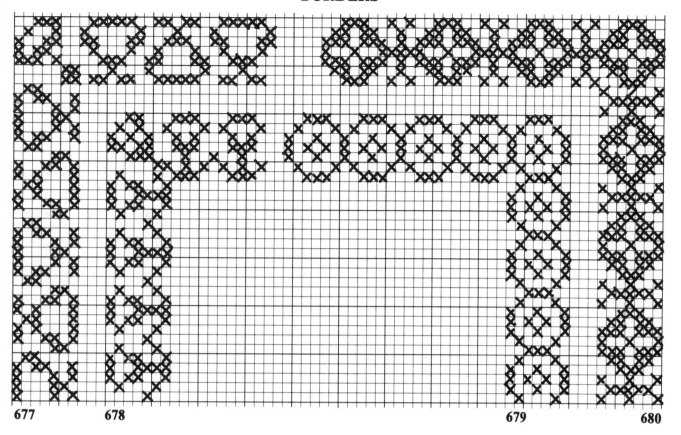

677 678 679 680

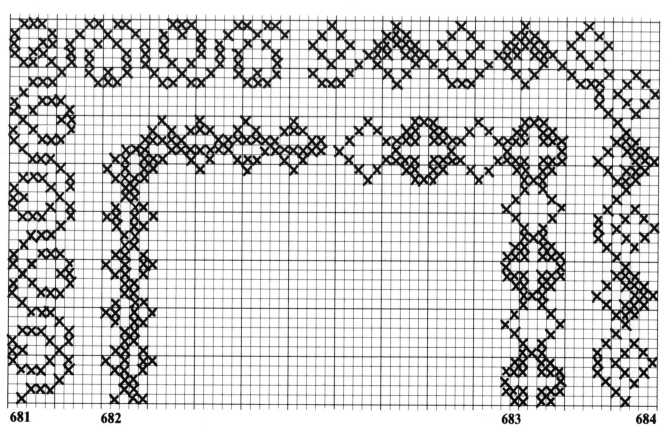

681 682 683 684

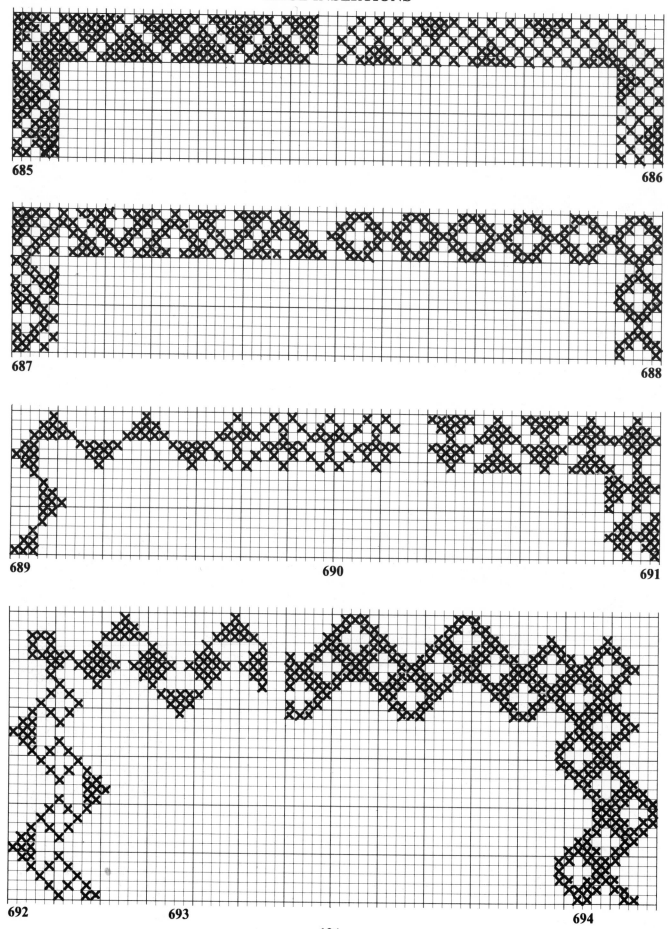

685

686

687

688

689

690

691

692

693

694

Designs 686 and 688 Dotted Swiss was used as a natural graph, each flock (dot) being the center of an imaginary square.

Designs 687 and 691 The waffle weave construction of this fabric determined the size of the Cross Stitch.

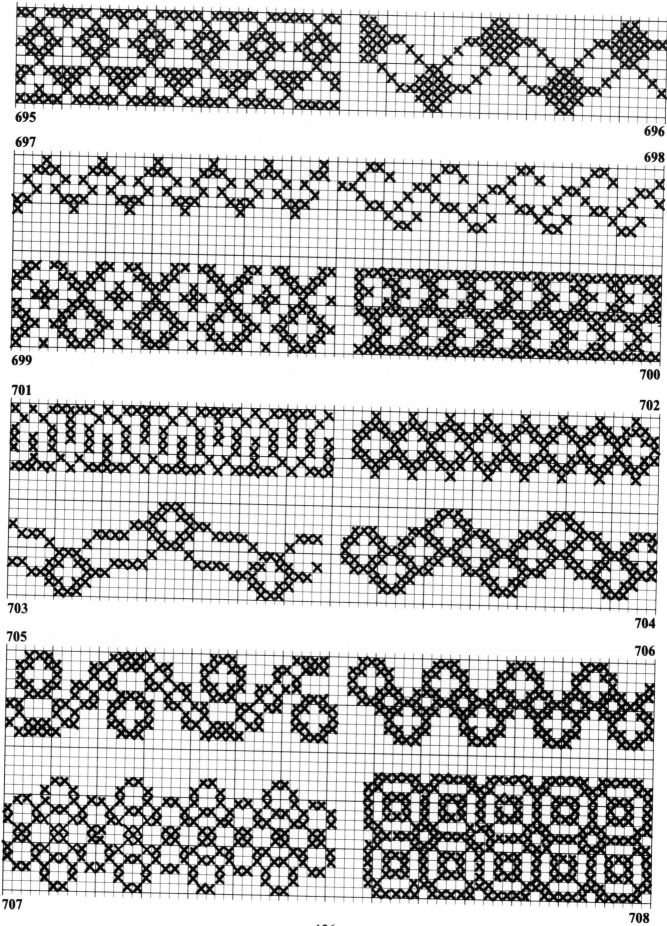

695

696

697

698

699

700

701

702

703

704

705

706

707

708

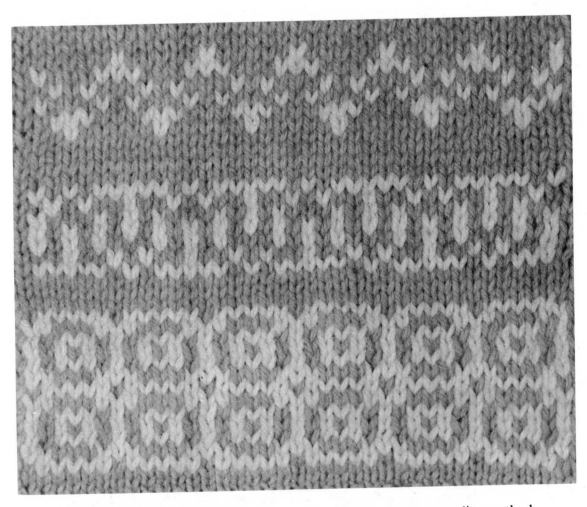

Designs 697, 701 and 708 Designs were knitted, using the stranding method (unused strand of yarn carried across wrong side of knitting).

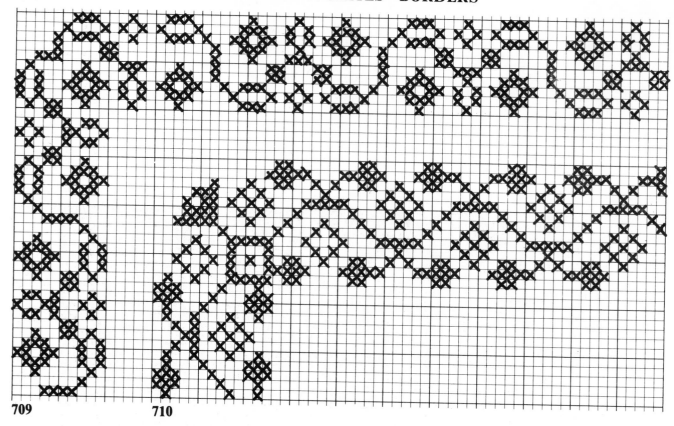

709   710

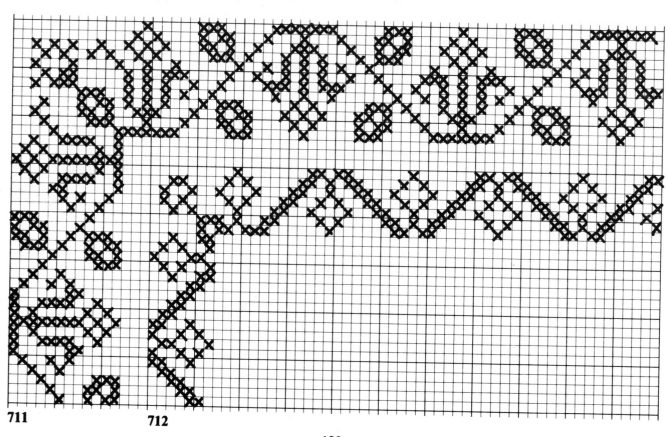

711   712

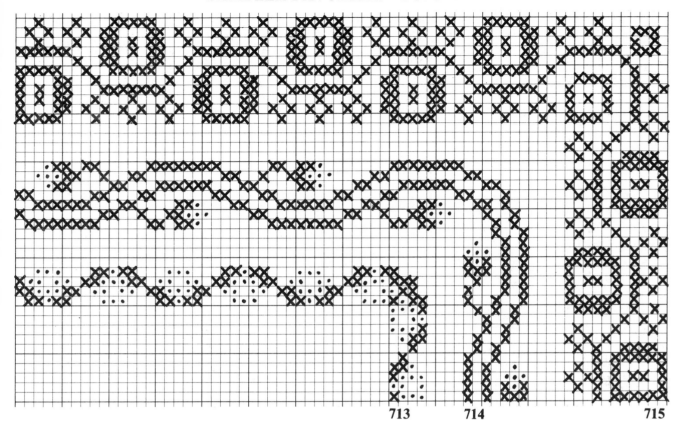

713   714   715

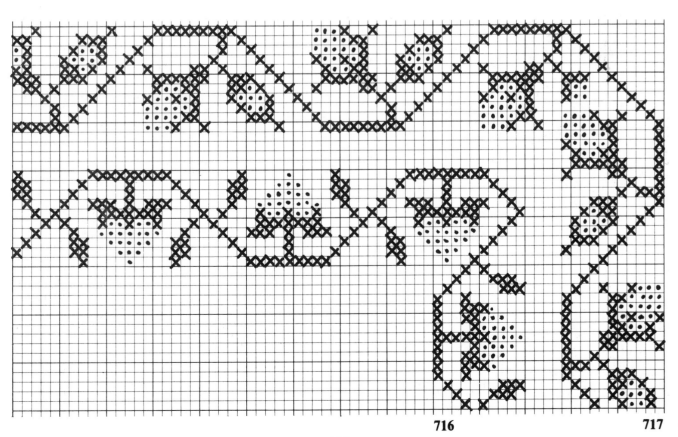

716   717

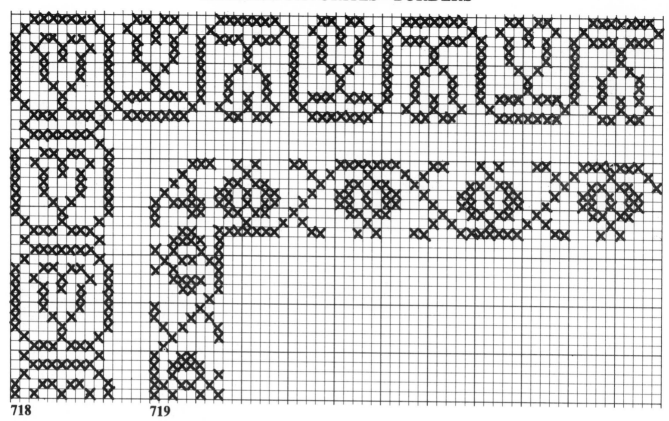

718 719

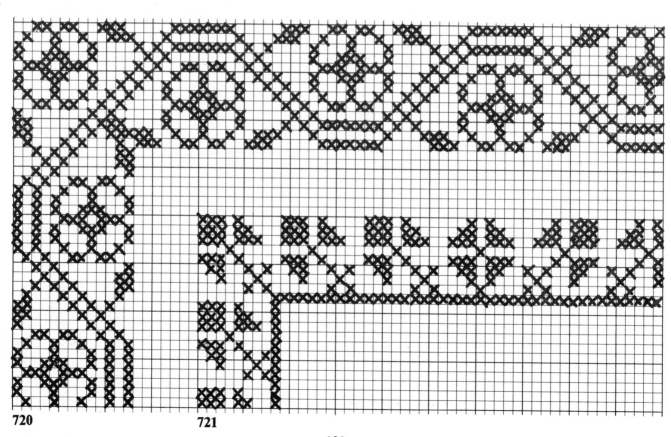

720 721

722

723

724

725

726

727

728

729

730

Design 729 Transfer or iron method is shown here. Design was drawn on tracing paper over a sheet of graph paper, then retraced over a sheet of carbon paper, carbon side up.

Left hand side of photograph shows the tracing paper pinned to the fine linen fabric.

Center section shows the stamped fabric after ironing. Right hand portion was worked with Embroidery Floss.

731

732

733

734

735

736

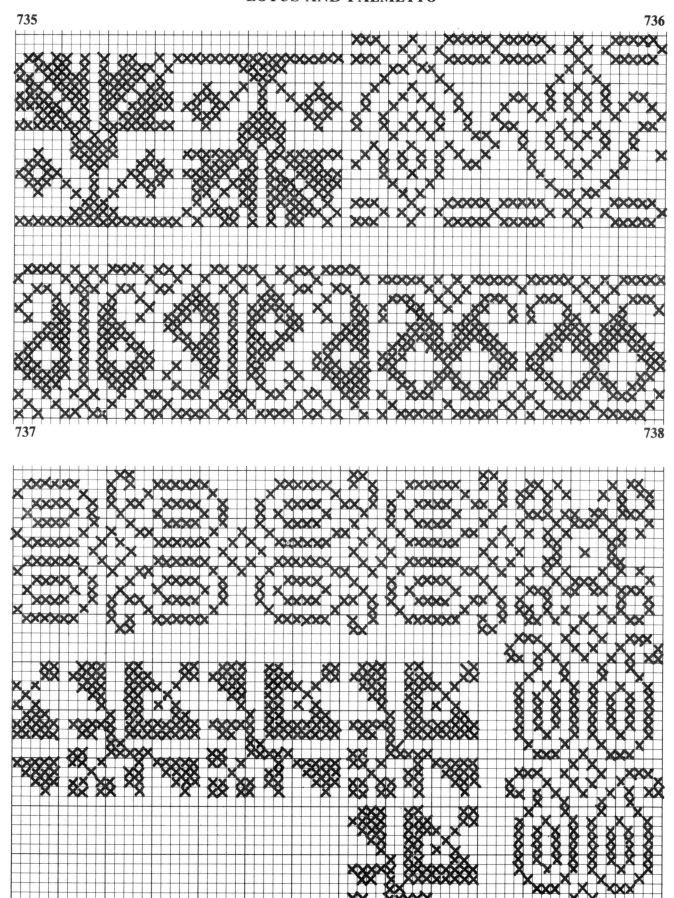

737

738

739

740

741   742   743   744

745   746

747

748   749

750

751

752

753   754   755

756

757

758   759

760   761

762

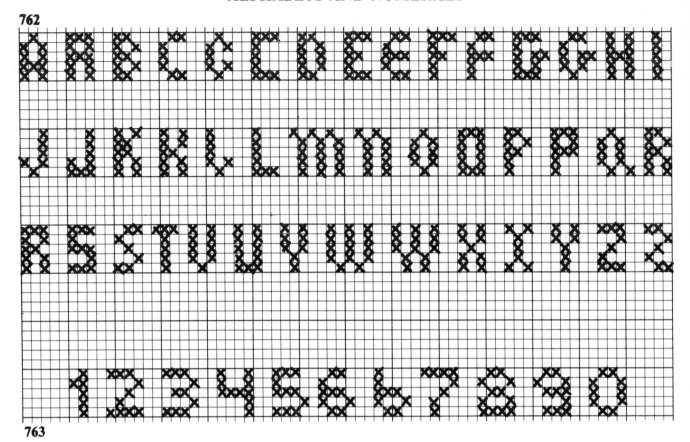

763

764

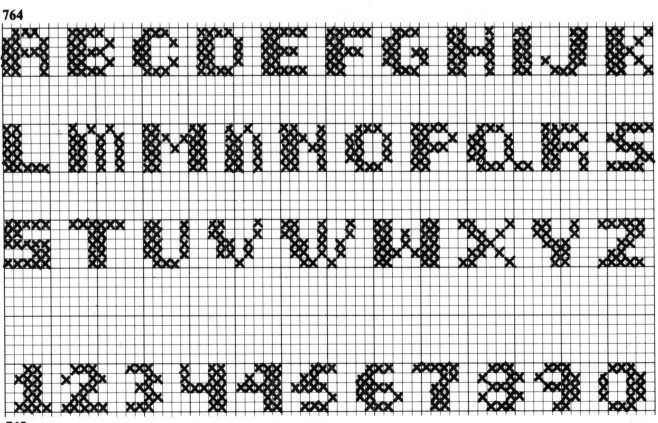

765

766

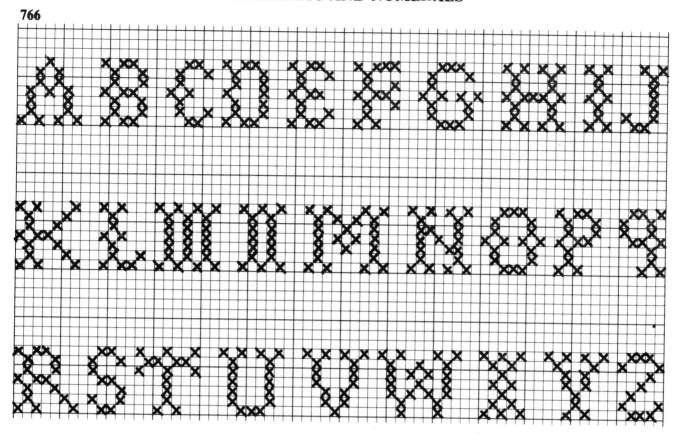

767

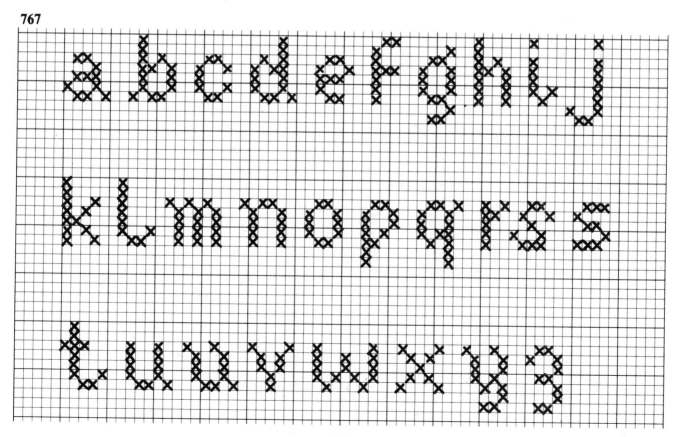

768

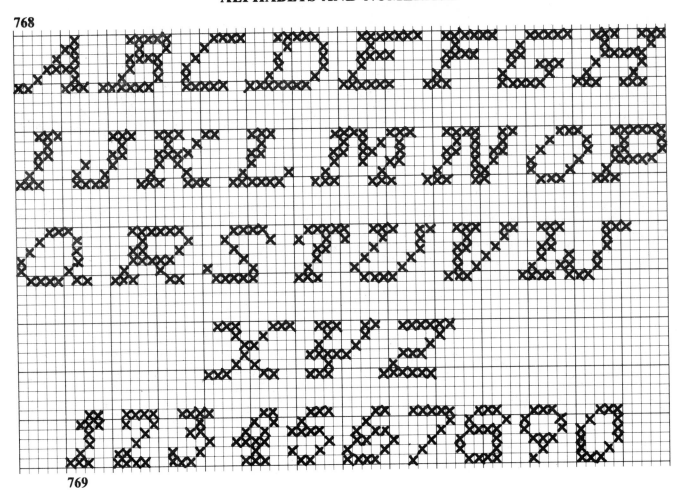

769

770

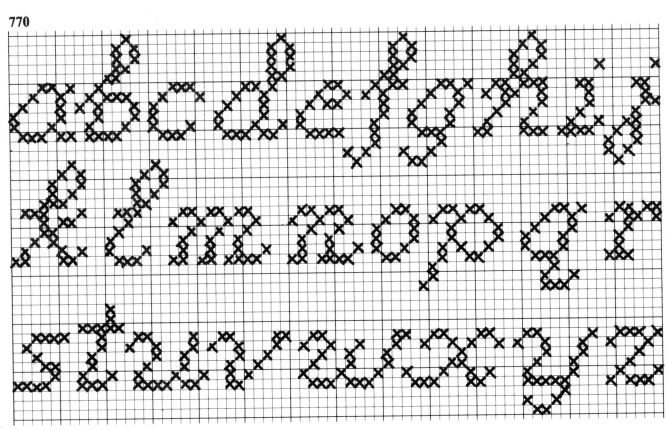

771

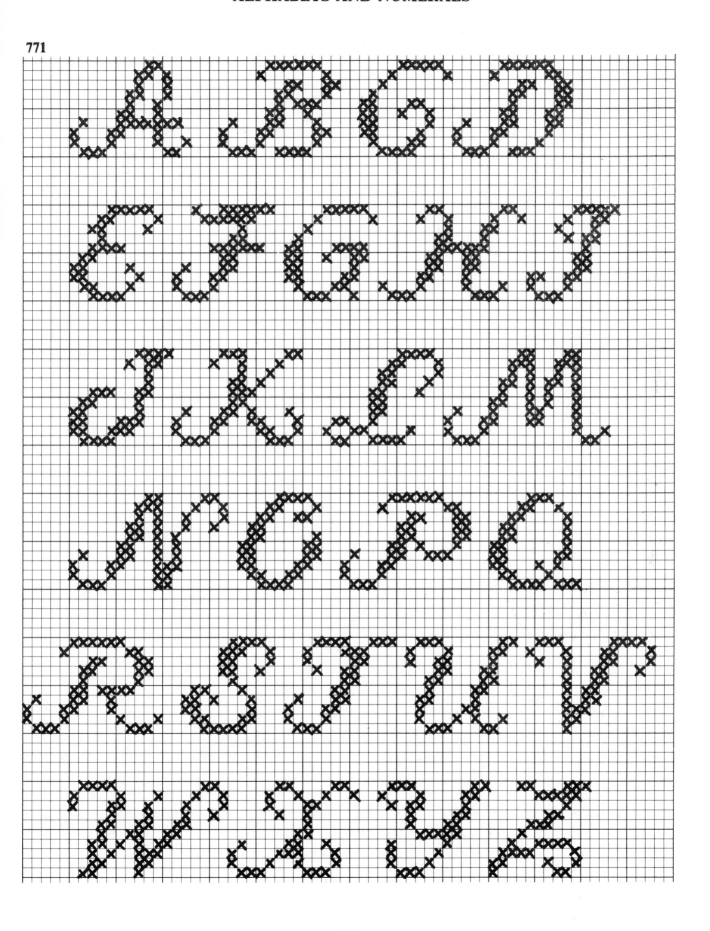

772

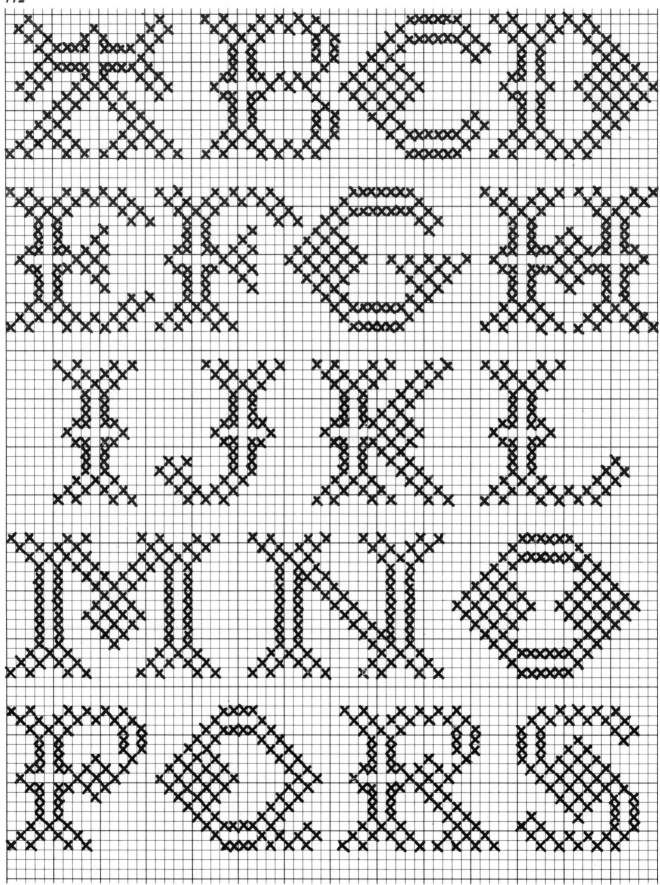

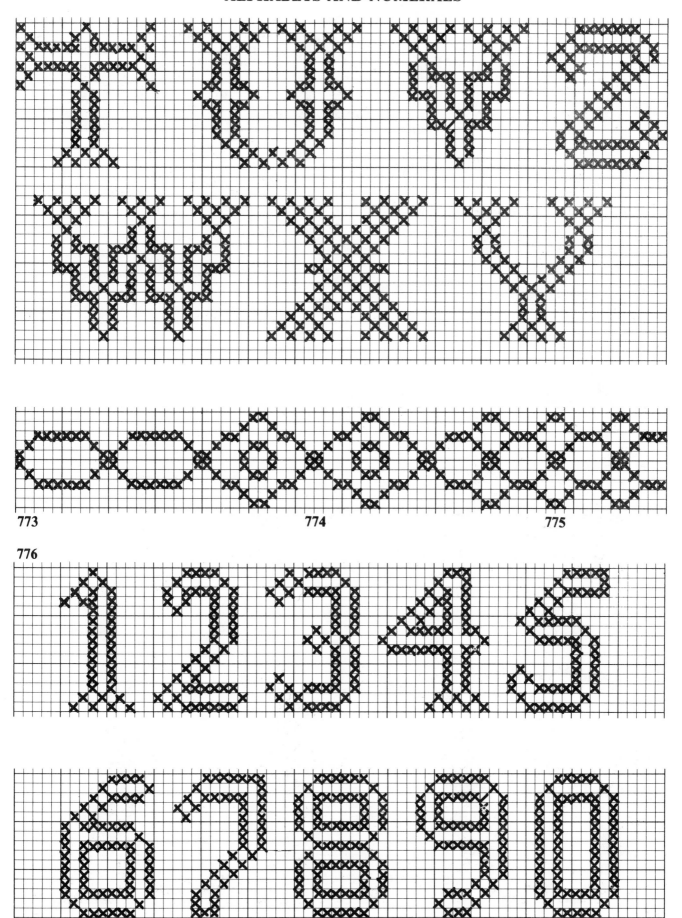

773   774   775

776

Design 179 Embroidery Floss on linen crash, two thread count.

Design 185 Wool yarn on burlap, two thread count.

An initial or monogram may be small or large, framed or unframed to suit taste, fabric, and project.

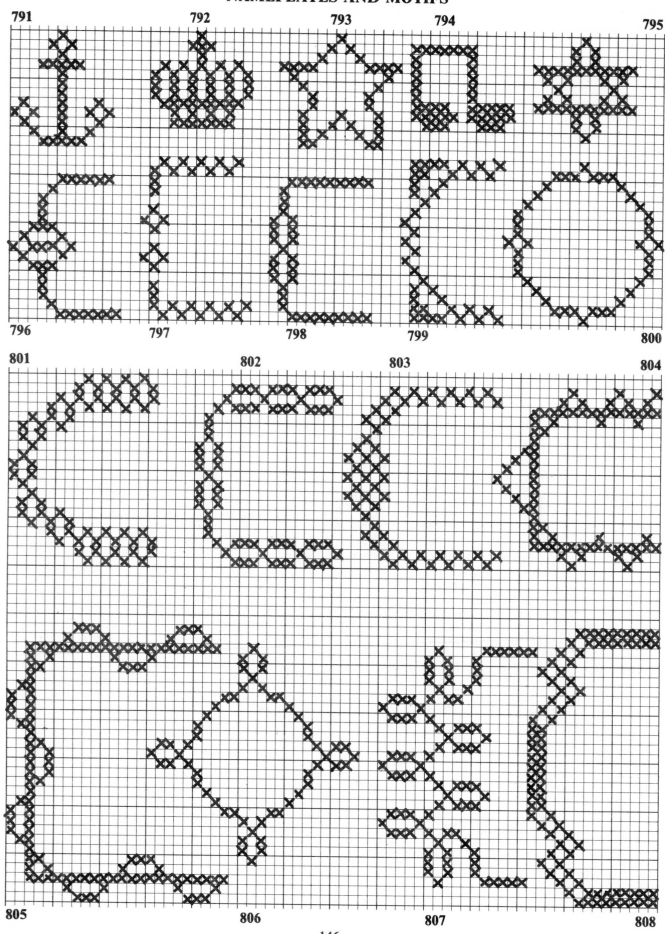

791   792   793   794   795
796   797   798   799   800
801   802   803   804
805   806   807   808

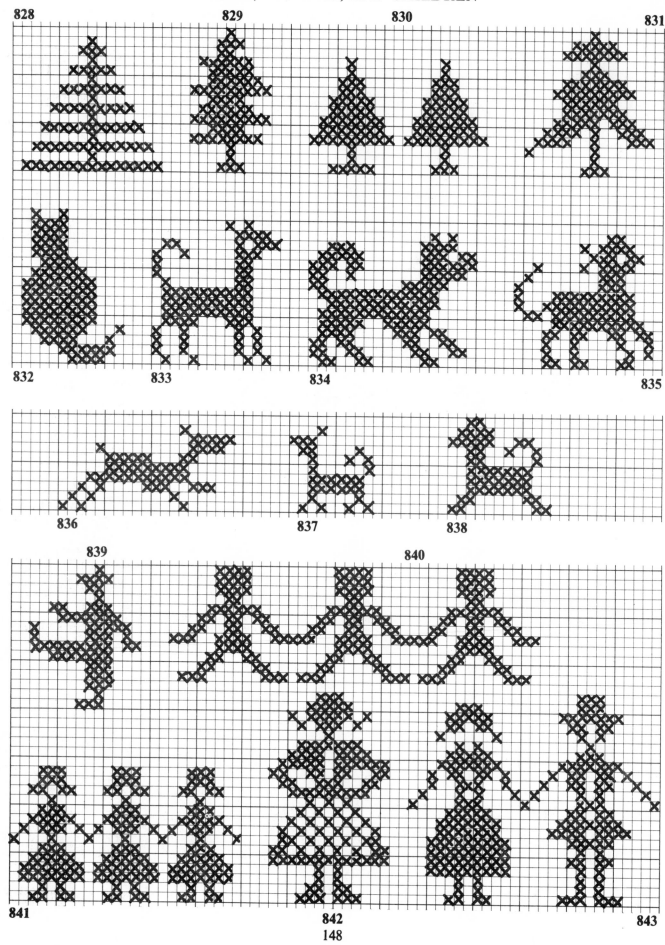

Design 541 Cross Stitch on an Afghan Stitch ground.

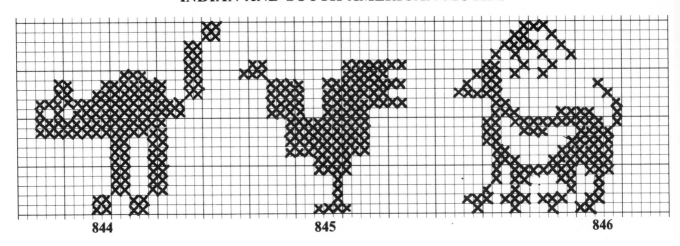

844 845 846

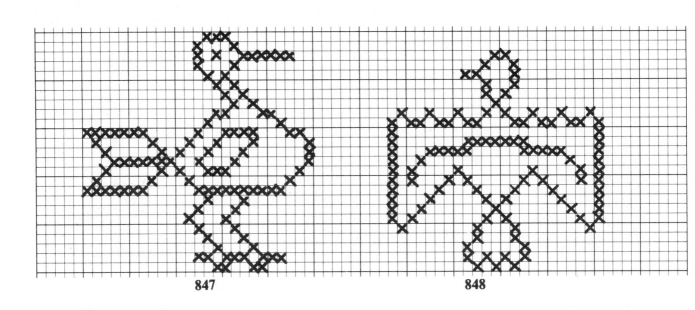

847 848

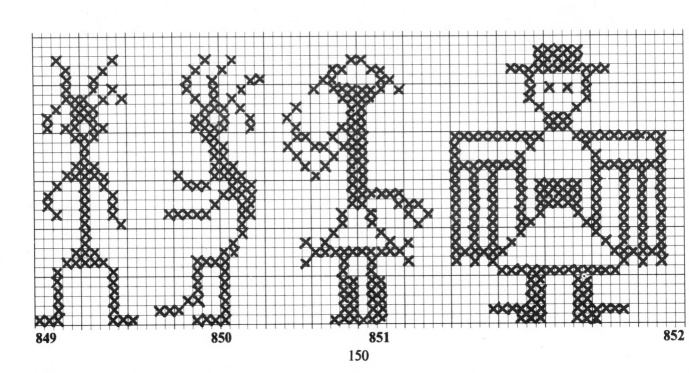

849 850 851 852

853

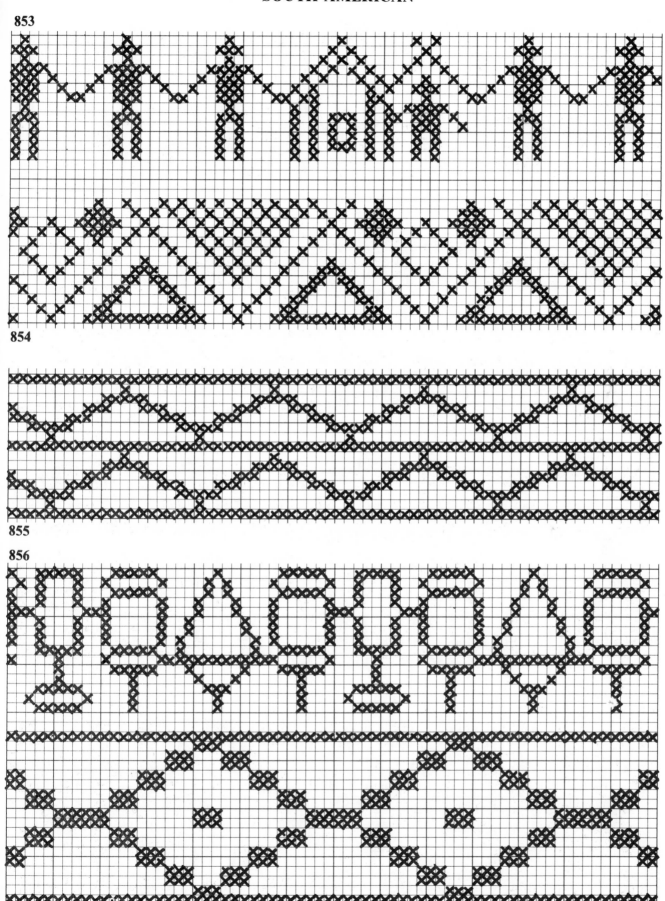

854

855

856

857

858

859

860

861

862

863

864

865

866

867

868

869

870

871

872

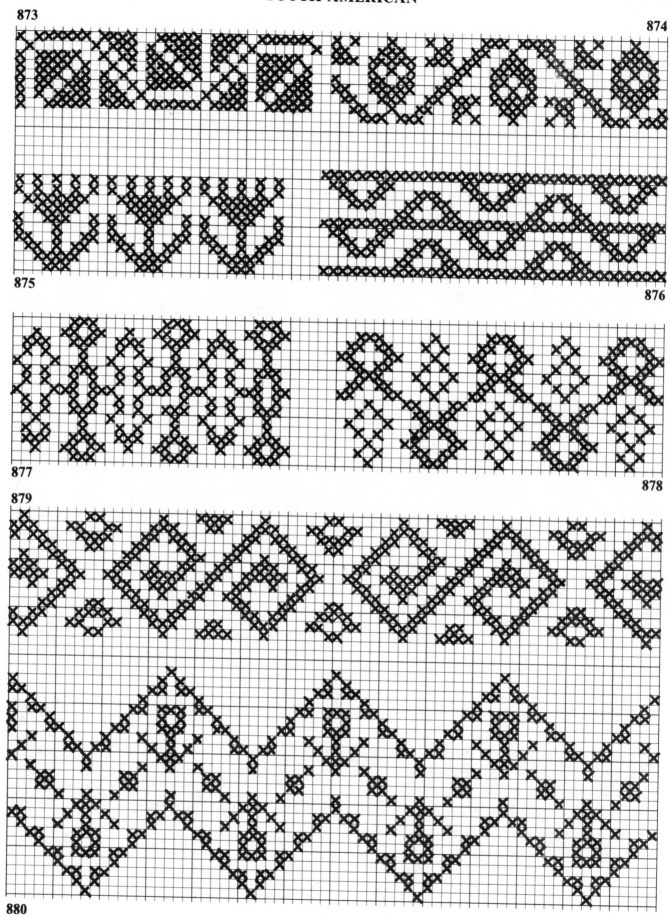

881

882

883

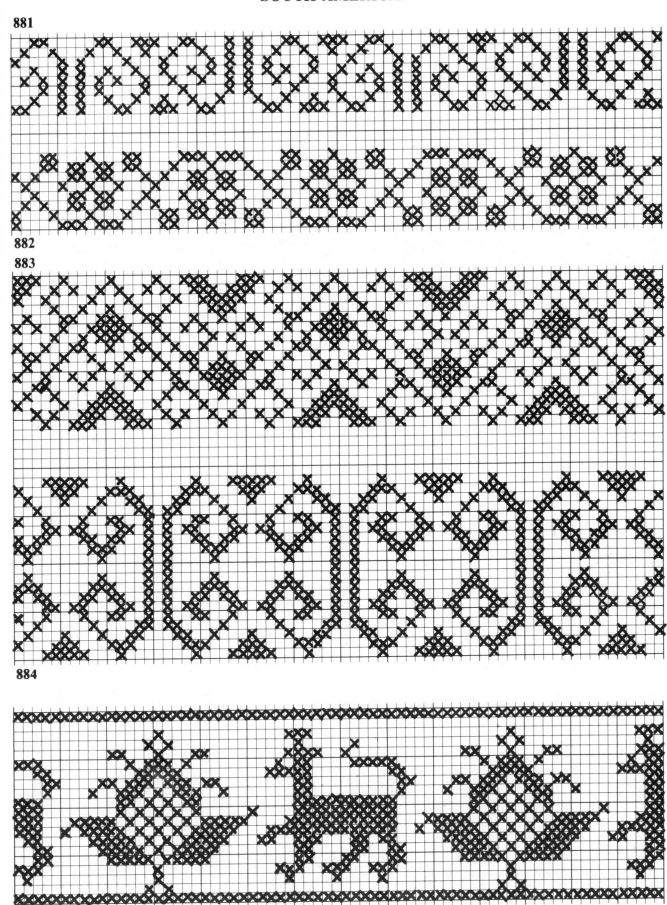

884

885

886

887

888

889

890

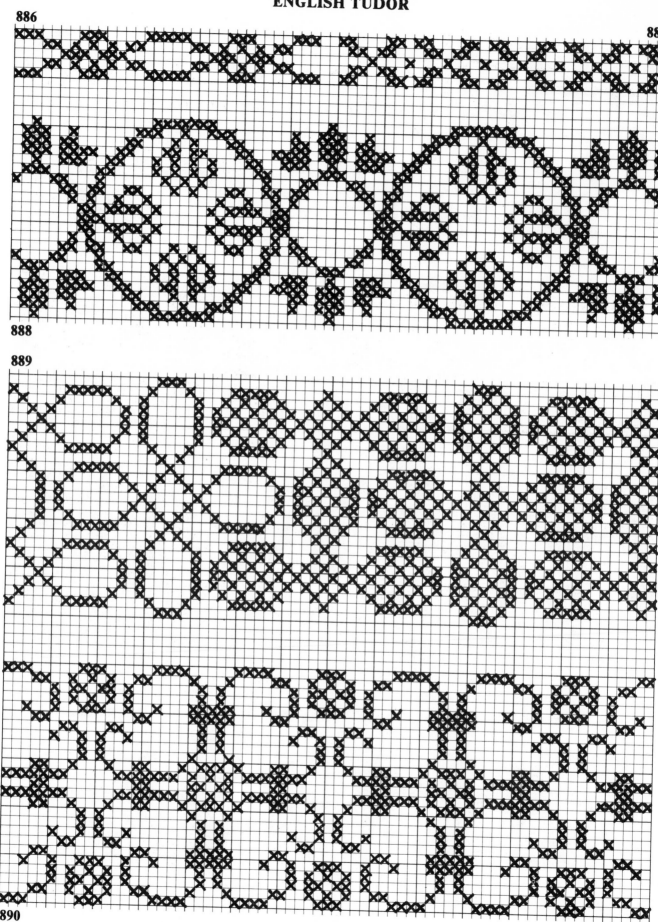

Designs 886, 887, and 889 Silk thread was used to cross stitch over 16 to-an-inch canvas covering a piece of hand-woven Thai silk. This is a method commonly used for working on closely woven materials.

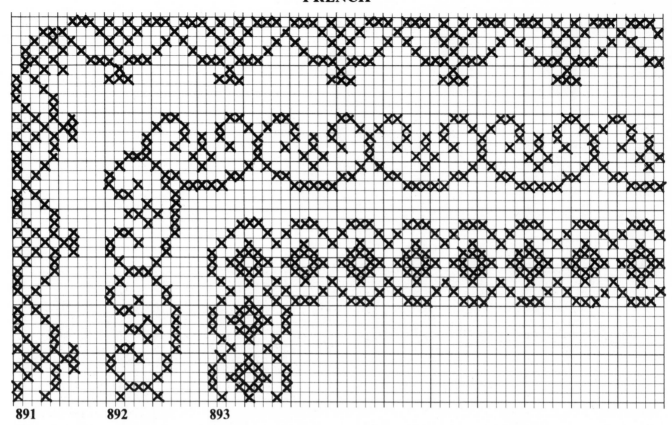

891   892   893

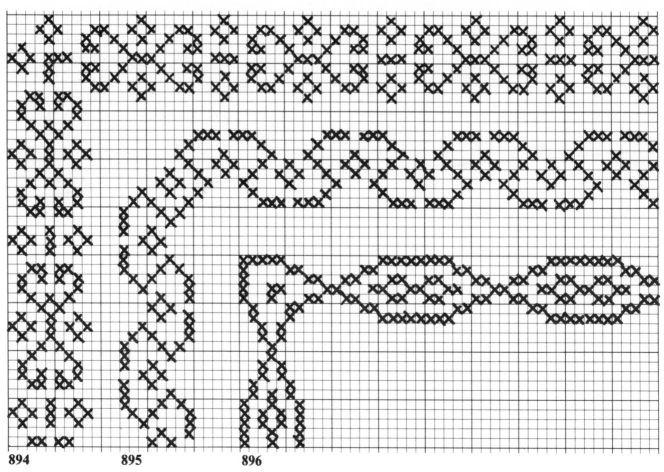

894   895   896

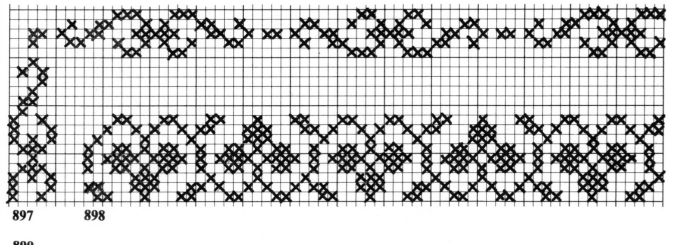

897   898

899

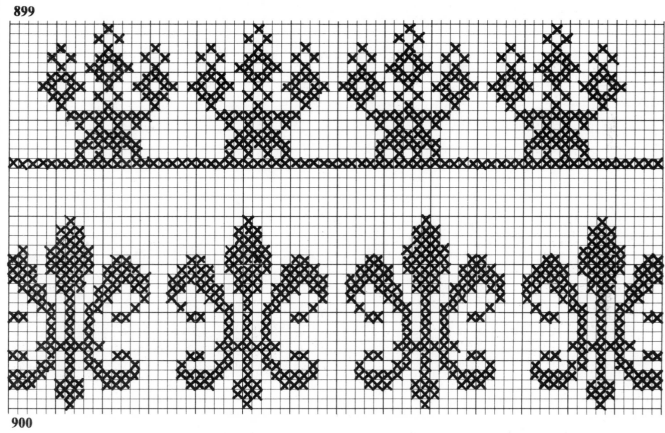

900

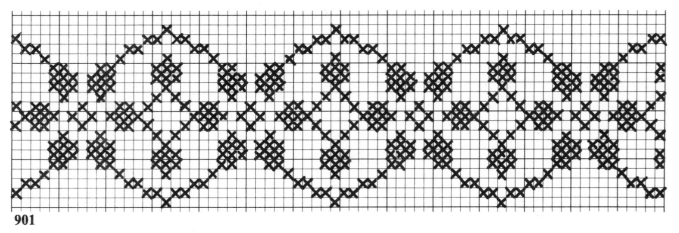

901

Designs 902 and 907 Duplicate Stitch on knitted ground, a method more suitable for multicolored designs than the stranding or knitting-in process.

926

927

928

929

930

931

932

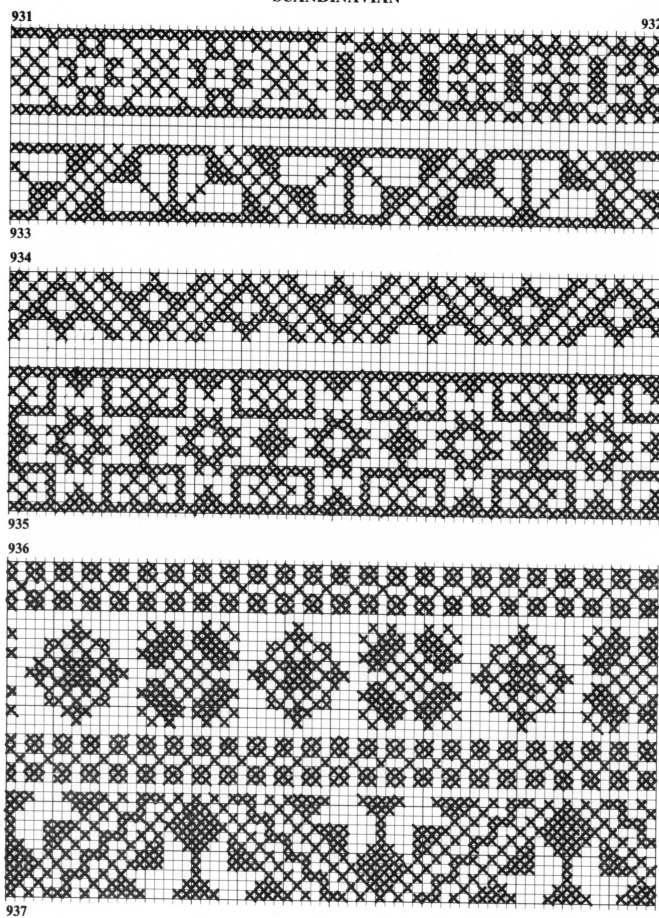

933

934

935

936

937

938

939

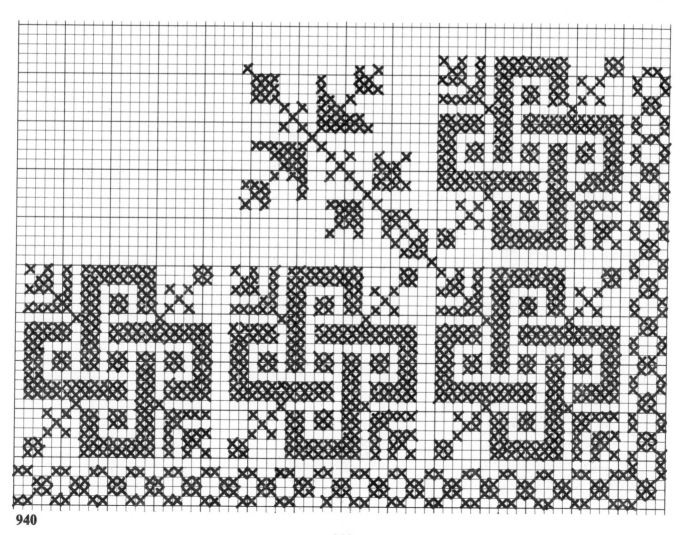

940

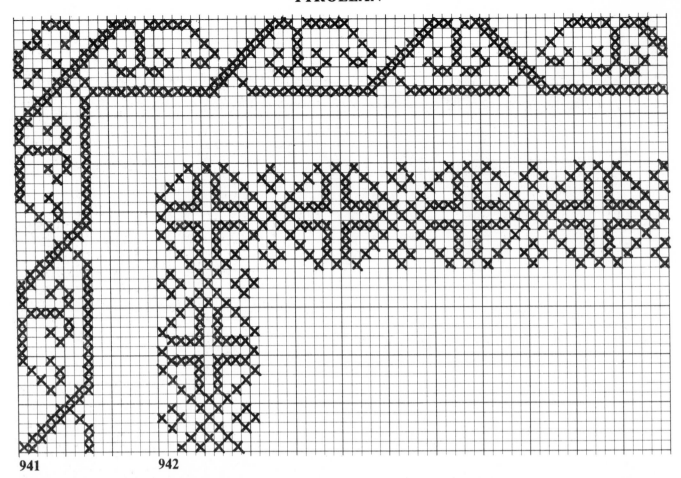

941   942

943

944

945

946

947

948

949

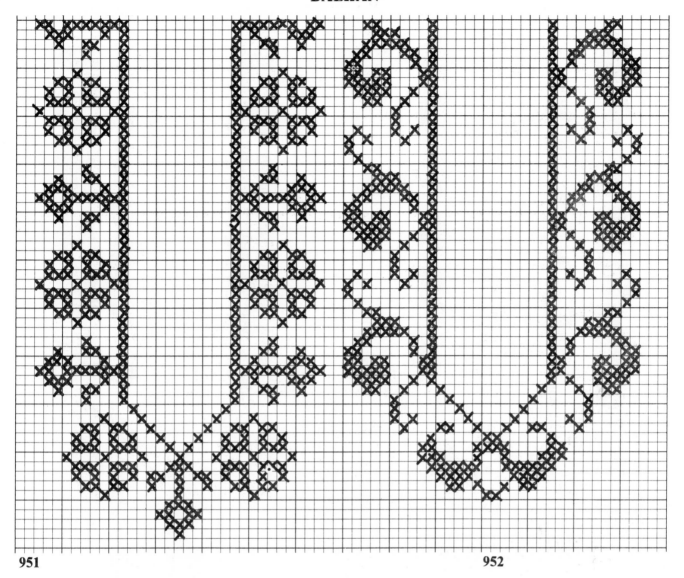

951

952

953

954

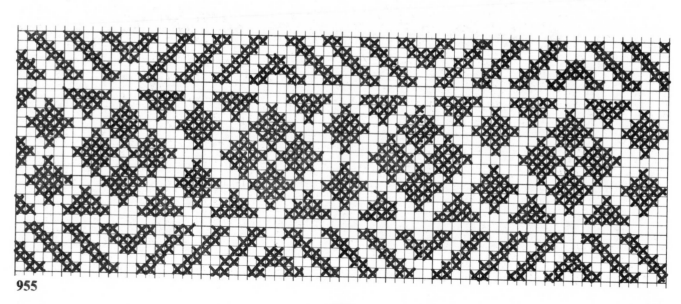

955

956

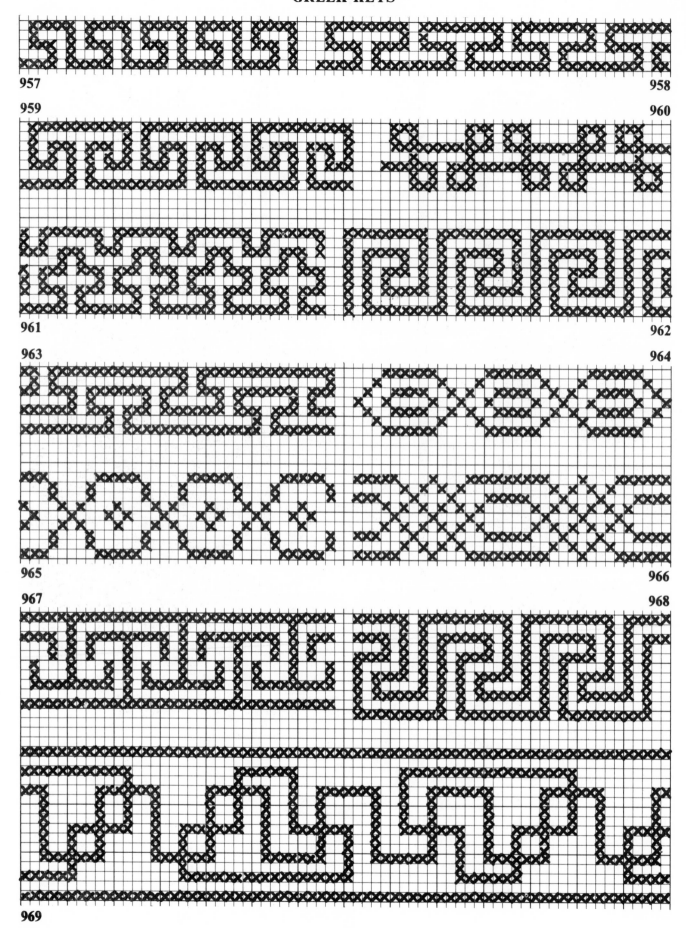

957

958

959

960

961

962

963

964

965

966

967

968

969

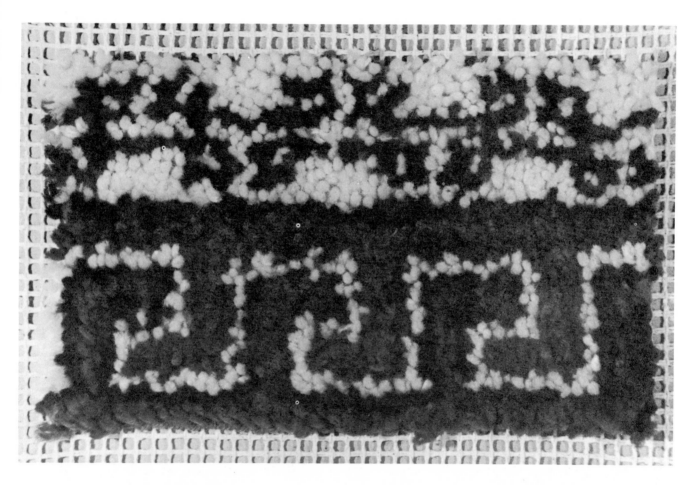

Designs 960 and 968 Rug yarn on very coarse canvas. Cut yarn and latch needle were used to make this sample, but other knotting and hooking techniques could be used.

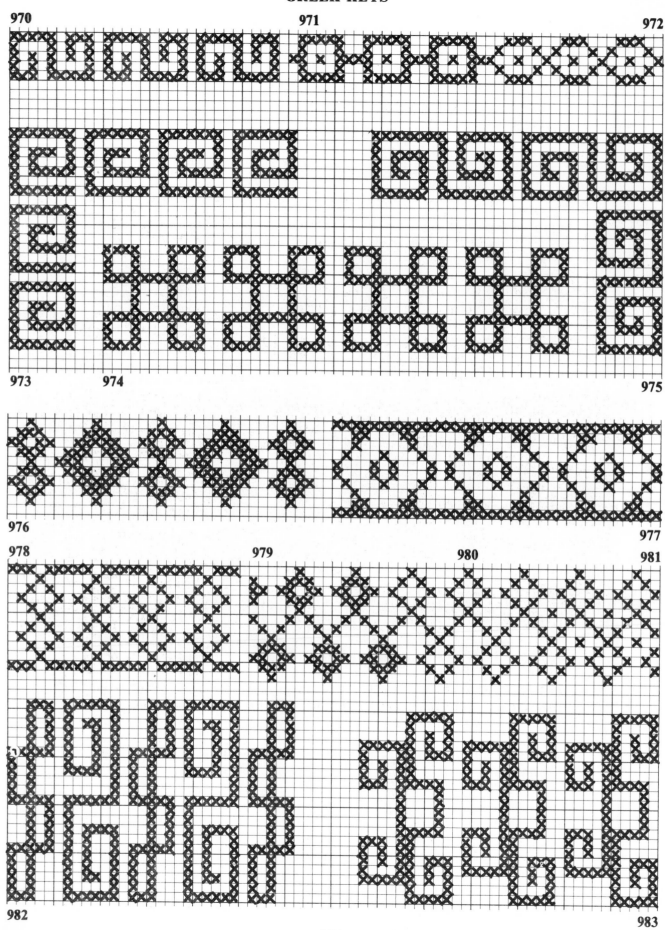

970   971   972
973   974   975
976   977
978   979   980   981
982   983

Designs 978, 970, and 976 Wool yarn worked over Monks cloth for fast, bold decorating.

984
985
986
987
988
989
990
991
992
993

Designs 988 and 991 Two color knitting, stranding method.

Cross Stitch graphs may be turned 90° and executed vertically in stitchery or knitting.

994

995

996

997

998

999

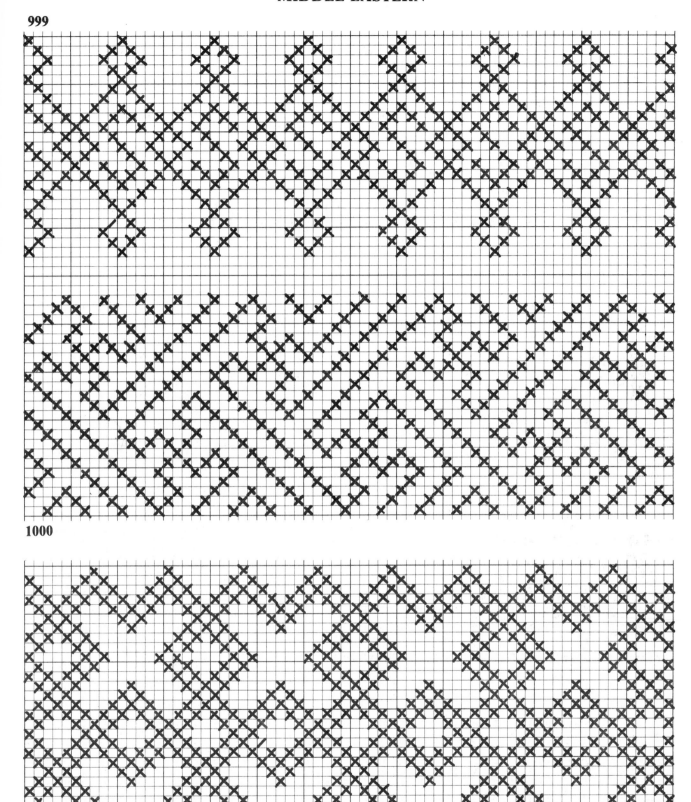

1000

1001

Bibliography

BORSSUCK, B. *97 Needlepoint Alphabets.* Arco Publishing Company, Inc., New York, 1975.

DREESMANN, CÉCILE. *Samplers for Today.* Van Nostrand Reinhold Company, New York, 1972.

DYE, DANIEL SHEETS. *Chinese Lattice Designs.* Dover Publications, Inc., New York, 1974.

Encyclopedia of Needlework. Hearthside Press, New York, 1963.

FORIS, MARIA and ANDREA. *Charted Folk Designs for Cross Stitch Embroidery.* Dover Publications, Inc., New York, 1975.

HALL, CARRIE A. and KRETSINGER, ROSE G. *The Romance of the Patchwork Quilt in America.* Crown Publishers, New York, 1935.

JUSTEMA, WILLIAM. *The Pleasures of Pattern.* Reinhold Book Corp., New York, 1968.

LANTZ, SHERLEE and LANE, MAGGIE A. *A Pageant of Pattern for Needlepoint Canvas.* Grosset and Dunlap, Inc., New York, 1975.

LIEBETRAU, PREBEN. *Oriental Rugs in Color.* Macmillan Publishing Co., New York, 1963.

SABINE, ELLEN S. *Early American Decorative Patterns.* Van Nostrand Reinhold Co., New York, 1958.

SCHIFFER, MARGARET B. *Historical Needlework of Pennsylvania.* Charles Scribner's Sons, New York, 1958.

WHITEFORD, ANDREW HUNTER. *North American Indian Arts.* Golden Press, New York, 1970.